Entertaining Bridge

Social Bridge at Home

How to start playing good Rubber Bridge
with minimum conventions
and maximum enjoyment

Caroline Salt

Illustrated by Elissa Kelly

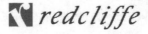 *redcliffe*

First published in 2007 by Redcliffe Press Ltd,
81G Pembroke Road
Clifton
Bristol BS8 3EA

E: info@redcliffepress.co.uk
www.redcliffepress.co.uk

ISBN 978-1-904537-74-8

British Library Cataloguing-in-Publication data
A catalogue record for this book is available from the British Library.

Published by Redcliffe Press Ltd, Bristol
Typeset by Harper Phototypesetters Ltd, Northampton
Cover design by eandp, Bath
Printed and bound by MPG Books, Bodmin, Cornwall

COMHAIRLE CHONTAE ÁTHA CLIATH THEAS
SOUTH DUBLIN COUNTY LIBRARIES

COUNTY LIBRARY, TOWN CENTRE, TALLAGHT
TO RENEW ANY ITEM TEL: 462 0073
OR ONLINE AT www.southdublinlibraries.ie

Items should be returned on or before the last date below. Fines, as displayed in the Library, will be charged on overdue items.

30/11/10		
12/12/11		
17/7/12		
26/2/14		
10/10		
6/11		

I dedicate this publication to all my pupils – past, present, and those to come. And to my two wonderful partners who have both enjoyed playing bridge for fun –
Royce and Geoff.

C.S.

Bridge.

HassaII

Acknowledgements

I would like to thank all those many people who have actively encouraged me in writing this book. In particular to my wonderful computer buff, Geoff Cutter, who has been comforting and patient and calmed me down when I threw up my hands and threatened to give up the whole idea!

To Lorna and David O'Brien for reading through the Bridge and recipes and helpfully correcting errors.

To Lorna O'Brien, Ann Bulman, Judy Chilton, Jenny Lomas and Ida Kraft for recipes.

To John McLeod for his permission to print his text for 'Honeymoon Bridge'.
His web site is www.pagat.com/boston/honeymoon.html

To Jonathan Goodall for doing such diligent research in order to compile the learned History of Bridge.

To Elissa Kelly, whose amusing drawings have highlighted so many of the points that I was eager to make.

Every effort has been made to trace the executors of the late John Hassall in order to obtain permission to print his illustrations, but without success. There is no wish to infringe copyright. I am grateful to Sarah Arthur for the loan of her mother's old score pad, from which Hassall's illustrations have been taken.

And, finally, to Peter George for his many hours of patient editing, and for the encouragement and support of Peter and his wife Harriet.

Contents

Introduction

The aim of bridge players is not always to join a Bridge Club. Yet that is automatically assumed by most writers of books written about the game, Bridge columnists, and Duplicate Bridge players. A tremendous number of players throughout the world meet in each other's homes enjoying Rubber Bridge for the social occasion – the friendly atmosphere, the chit-chat, all mixed with the undoubted stimulus of playing the best game in the world.

Often a snack or a meal is an integral part of this entertaining; Bridge can be played in the morning (coffee time), in the afternoon (lunch or tea), or in the evening (supper or dinner). It can be informal – "bring your own sandwiches", or it can be formal – dinner jackets and two or three tables. It is just an extraordinarily pleasant way of passing the time, with enough jolly talk during mealtimes and in the pauses between hands, but always with everyone's eagerness to 'get back to the cards'!

This book is not just a series of lessons. As Bridge is such a social game, at the end of this book various recipes for hosting lunch, tea, or supper are suggested. Also there are ideas for holding a Bridge party with two or more tables, which could include charity fundraising.

Bridge can be played by all ages – some schools offer bridge amongst their activities. Also, remember that as we get older, the more athletic sports can become curtailed. Bridge can be played for ever. I have partnered efficient players who suffer from Alzheimer's, but seem to be able to remember their card sense; and played with Braille cards for a friend whose sight was definitely failing. It is a wonderful game for anyone who is on their own – they are able to play with so many different people in so many different places – it can provide a whole new dimension.

Rubber Bridge players are not inferior beings who have been unable to rise to the dizzy heights of Club play – most of us have simply decided that we do not play a game in order to *win* and to gain status by improving our Master Point tally. We play for fun.

The vast majority of Bridge Clubs play Duplicate Bridge. This is when each couple plays the same cards, which are handed on in a 'wallet', and thus the luck of one partnership getting good cards and their opponents picking up useless ones is taken away. The scores are worked out so that the winners are not your normal opponents, but the other players who were sitting in the same direction as you at their tables. The excitement and, yes, the fear, certainly makes for an adrenalin rush – but against this is the fact that there can sometimes be an unfriendly atmosphere since everyone is intent on only one thing: Winning! Talking is often discouraged, introductions can be at the minimum and play is probably faster than social bridge players find comfortable. Generally, you do not go to a Duplicate Bridge Club to make new friends, although I generalise, as there are some very pleasant and companionable clubs.

If you are playing in a Bridge Club and, therefore, probably playing Duplicate, you usually stay with the same partner for every session. You and your partner have worked out how you will bid in order to suit you both. You know, say, that if she bids "2 Clubs" it does not mean that she likes Clubs, but is a point count. A joint system has been established – you could have decided that if you chewed your right thumb it meant 'go for a slam' – but, of course, that would be cheating!

These 'odd' ways of bidding are called 'Conventions' and they are not rules, they are merely ways of deciding what you and your partner think will be the best contract. Suits or numbers may be bid which mean something other than their face value. Some 'conventions' are necessary and I will be teaching you a very few of them; they are extremely useful, if both you and your partner understand and use them correctly, but otherwise they could be muddling and lead to a disastrous conclusion!

I have a friend who is a good simple player (and what is wrong about that?); however she can never remember the word 'conventions' and talks instead about 'contraptions'. She obviously associates them with extra difficulties – something 'hung onto' the game and not strictly necessary in her, and in many other rubber bridge players' eyes – just adding complications.

If you are at the start of your Bridge learning, everything that I have written about 'bidding' or even 'suits', not to mention those 'contraptions', is as clear as mud. But do not panic – this will be kept simple and you will be amazed how soon you can actually have fun with the game. My aim is to make you an excellent player, simply because you are not having to pile too much additional information into your brain!

If you, like me, enjoy social Bridge, you will play with many other people – some good, some only adequate – but you will appreciate that a beginner will only improve by playing the game as often as possible. Some will have learned many different conventions, some hardly any – it really seems more sensible to pare down to the minimum the knowledge we have to accumulate in order to be able to play the game at all. Thus, if you are pitted against a 'convention freak' you can say, 'I'm afraid that I only play very simple bridge'. Your partner may be disappointed but, when she sees how well you bid and play your game, without the necessity of Drury, Lebensohl, Michaels or the rest, she will appreciate that you really *do* know your bridge.

There are Bridge Clubs where Rubber Bridge is played for vast sums. It is rumoured that people were declared bankrupt simply through losing at Bridge, and in the 1930s when Bridge was at its height, people like Edward VIII always gambled when playing. Nowadays, when playing socially, very few play for money: sometimes a penny a point, or a matchstick – but, the game's the thing not the reward!

This book will give you the essential information that you, as beginners, need: it includes a few conventions, but *very* few – and keeps you revising what you have learned. All the effort that others strive to remember in order to play the more abstruse conventions can be used by you thoroughly to know and understand your game. So, if anyone asks you if you can play, you will be able to say 'Yes I *can*'!

I would suggest that you don't rush indigestibly through this book. Study each lesson and absorb it before you move on to the next. You will find that things are constantly repeated – just in case you need revision. The best way of using the examples throughout is to lay out all four hands (North, East, South, West), and then work out what *you* would bid and how the play would go.

Even though you may not have enough players to make up a complete table, I have included Bridge for two and three players towards the end of this book, so that you can keep practising. If you are on your own, the best thing to do is to deal out four hands and pretend that you are all four players, bidding and playing all the hands.

By the way, in this age of political correctness, we are very conscious of sexual discrimination so throughout I have made the partnership sitting North/South 'He' and the partnership sitting East/West 'She'. Hopefully, that is fair enough!

As a qualified bridge teacher, although not of strict Acol Bridge, I have been teaching Rubber Bridge for many years and this book is the result of being aware and listening to the many different comments made by the hundreds of my pupils endeavouring and succeeding to master the basic elements of this most wonderful game.

1

How to start

You are learning a simplified form of Acol Bridge, which I have always used in teaching beginners. 'Acol' Bridge is so called after a bridge club in the 1930s which was in a road in London called 'Acol Street'. This is where this particular bidding system came into being, and, although there is really no 'Standard Acol' system, this is used by a number of competent players, who started off – just like you – as beginners. It is Contract Bridge because you *contract* (you promise hopefully) to win a specified number of tricks.

It is played by four people. Two playing as partners against the other two. Partners sit opposite each other and are known as North/South and East/West. Your partner (while you are playing and while you are discussing your game afterwards) is your very best friend – you must *always* be polite and friendly and if you must criticise do so very gently and only if they want you to help When you finish playing, thank your partner and say "Wasn't that a good game!" – encouragement works wonders!

For this game, you do not need expensive equipment: just four chairs, a card table, preferably two packs of cards, pencils and score pads (but you could play on the floor with an old pack of cards, a pencil stub and the back of an envelope!). Of course, when you get 'hooked', presents will never be a problem: a card table, bridge cloth, numerous double packs of cards, bridge mugs, special pencils – the list is endless!

There are fifty-two cards in a pack – the joker is not used, unlike Canasta. There are four suits of thirteen cards each: Spades, Hearts, Diamonds, Clubs. The Ace is the highest and the two is the lowest. The top five cards in each suit – A, K, Q, J, 10 – are called Honour cards or Honours; there are, therefore, 20 Honour cards in the whole pack.

Unless you have arranged to play with someone before the game, it is usual to draw for partners. The pack is spread out, face down, on the table; each player picks a card (not from the last few at each end). The two higher cards play as partners against the two lower cards. If two cards of the same rank are turned up, then the card in the higher suit has won: the highest suit is Spades, then Hearts, then Diamonds, then Clubs.

May I Play?   Hassall

For instance: Mary, John, David and Catherine are drawing for partners. Mary picks the first card, followed by John, then David and Catherine. Who plays together when these cards are turned up?

1) King Spades, 3 Spades, 3 Clubs, Ace Diamonds.
2) 5 Hearts, Jack Diamonds, Queen Clubs, Jack Spades.
The answer to (1) is Mary with Catherine and John with David.

The answer to (2) is David with Catherine and Mary with John.

The one who drew the highest card can choose on which seat they wish to sit and their partner sits opposite; one partnership will be called North/South and their opponents will be East/West. He also decides which pack of cards their side will use, and is the dealer of the first hand and the first one to bid – that is, to choose how many tricks he thinks they can win.

This is complicated to start with but is a way of showing that you know how to play Rubber Bridge!

The cards that have been chosen are shuffled ('made') by the person on the dealer's left; the dealer then passes them across himself to the person on his right for them to be 'cut' towards him, and he deals. This means that both of the dealer's opponents have had an opportunity to mix up the cards he will be dealing. Meanwhile, the dealer's partner shuffles the other pack of cards and places it on his right ('if you're not a fool quite, put the cards on your right'). When the next game is to be played, the dealer sitting clockwise passes the shuffled pack of cards across himself to the opponent on his right, who will then cut them before they are dealt. Once again the dealer will have a pack of cards that will have been shuffled and cut by his opponents.

The cards are then dealt out, face down, starting with the player on his left and in a clockwise direction until all fifty-two cards are dealt. Each player will receive 13 cards. The last card is dealt to the dealer.

Do not pick up your cards until they are all dealt – this is so that the dealer can have the same length of time to study his cards. Also, before turning over your cards, count them because sometimes an incorrect number of cards may have unwittingly been dealt.

When you do look at your cards, do not allow anyone else to see them – hold them in a fan shape in one hand and sort them into suits; generally red and black suits are grouped alternately because it is easier to differentiate between them; then sort each suit into order of rank – e.g. A, J, 10, 5, 3.

Counting Your High Card Points – 'HCP'
An Ace equals 4 points; a King equals 3; a Queen, 2; a Jack, 1. There are, therefore, forty points altogether in a pack. Both partnerships (North/South and East/West) need 12-13 points to start the bidding; to reply to your partner once he or she has opened, you need at least 6 points.

2

The Bidding

In Bridge, the actual number of points in your hands is not mentioned aloud. You will make one or more bids which will say what you hold. This is why you have to be as accurate as possible. Play is preceded by the bidding (also called 'the auction') and the one who bids the highest will win the right to play the hand.

The aim in bidding is to state how good your cards are; to establish which suit you wish to be Trumps and therefore superior over the other three suits; or if you have even distribution of cards in the suits and 12-14 points, to call '1 No Trump'. 'Even distribution' means not having only one card in a suit, 'a singleton'; nor having a good 5 card Heart or Spade suit, because you and your partner might be happier playing with these suits as trumps.

Also, you need to work out how many tricks you can win when, or if, your partner bids. A trick is when all four players have each played one card in turn.

There are thirteen tricks in each game and when you are bidding, the first six tricks are discounted. How high one bids is the number of tricks to be won over and above those first six tricks. Therefore, if you bid '1' of a suit or No Trumps that would mean that you have contracted (hopefully promised your partner) that you can win 6 + 1 = 7 tricks; if you said '4' that would equal ten tricks. You cannot bid for less than '1' (seven tricks) and the most you can bid is '7', which would mean you have contracted to win all thirteen tricks.

The dealer makes the first bid, generally starting with a low bid, for example saying '1 Heart', meaning 'I contract to win 6 + 1 tricks, with Hearts as Trumps'. After the dealer has made his first bid, the player to the left makes their bid, and so on clockwise. Each player may say either "No Bid" or make a bid. Even though a player may have said "No Bid" once or even twice, they may still make a 'bid' or reply to their partner's bid, later in the auction. How high one bids is the number of tricks to be won over and above six tricks.

If all the players pass without making a bid, that hand is thrown in and the next dealer (clockwise) deals a new hand.

When any player makes the first bid, the auction has started and will be won by the partnership that bids the highest.

After a bid, any player at his turn may make a higher bid. A bid is higher than a previous bid if it is a larger number than the previous bid: e.g. 3 Diamonds is higher than 2 Spades. Or, if the bids are for the same number of tricks, the highest ranking wins, which is in this order: 'No Trumps' then Spades, Hearts, Diamonds, Clubs. Therefore, if one of your opponents bids 1 Heart and you wanted Diamonds to be trumps – you would have to say "2 Diamonds", but, if you liked Spades you could say '1 Spade', as it is higher ranking than the opponent's '1 Heart'.

If you have the right number of High Card Points (HCP), i.e. at least 12, you could start the bidding, or 'open' for your partnership. However, you must never bid a suit with only three cards, although you could later support your partner with that suit. If you only have 4 cards in a particular suit you should only bid it once; with 5 of more cards you could repeat the same suit. Length (the number of cards of the same suit) is more important than strength – 10, 8, 7, 6, 5 of trumps is better than King, Jack, 10, 9. If you hold 12-14 points and all the suits are equally good, then call No Trumps, although that would be unsuitable if you had a suit with only one card.

If your partner has opened the bidding for your side with, for instance, 1 Spade, you now know he has at least 12 points and at least 4 Spades. You could then reply to him

17

if you hold 6 points. If he then repeats his Spades, he has 5 of them. The auction is over once a bid is followed by three "No Bids" – in other words all the other players have passed.

Trumps

In Bridge, hands are played either in 'No Trumps', or in a 'Trump Suit'. The Trump Suit chosen and declared is either Spades, Hearts, Diamonds or Clubs. Each partnership is vying to win the bidding with their chosen suit as Trumps. It is important that between them the partners have, hopefully, 8 cards of their chosen Trumps. With these Trumps, they can take even an Ace of another suit with a 2 of the Trump suit, provided they don't hold any card in that Ace suit.

If, between them, the winning partnership's suits are equally good, they might decide to play the contract in 'No Trumps', meaning no one suit is particularly dominant and all four suits in both hands are equally balanced.

You should always try to be aware of what you might be able to bid on the next round. For example, supposing you pick up your hand and find that you have, say, 13 points and these consist of: Spades K, 2; Hearts K, 3, 2; Diamonds 9, 8, 7, 5, 4; Clubs A, Q, J. If you open your bidding with your 5 card suit (Diamonds), it is really not good enough to bid again, is it? Therefore, you should open with 1 No Trump and then for your second bid mention your Diamonds. This gives your partner more information and doesn't make him or her think that the Diamonds are a wonderful suit.

The person who has made the highest and last bid has decided the Trump suit (or No Trumps) by making that winning bid. If they have ended with 2 Spades, they have contracted to win 8 tricks with Spades as Trumps and will be the 'declarer' (the one who plays the hand), unless the partner has already bid the same suit earlier, then he will become the 'declarer' and the partner will be the 'dummy' (the one who lays down his cards on the table – after the first card has been played by the opponent on the declarer's left). The dummy's cards will be seen by everyone, so that the whole table are aware of 27 cards (their own, dummy's and the declarer's lead card). The problem (and the joy) of bridge is working out who of the other two players hold which cards.

Dummy.

Hassall

Remember, bidding is only a way of telling your partner what you have in your hand and listening to what your opponents have in their hands. Do remember that you are not playing on your own – *you have a Partner.* Always trust him or her.

Precis

In a suit contract: Open 1 Spade, Heart, Diamond or Club if you have 12-18 points
Partner may be able to reply with 6+ points

With even distribution, which means 4-3-3-3 suits, or 4-4-3-2, or even 5-3-3-2, or 5-4-2-2:

Open 1 No Trump if you have 12-14 points.
Open 1 No Trump even with a 5 card suit provided it is a minor suit and is relatively poor.

For example:
a) you hold Spades: Ace, 5, 2; Hearts: King, 4; Diamonds: 9, 7, 8, 3, 2; Clubs: Ace, Queen, 2.
   What should you bid as the opener?
b) you hold Spades: King, Jack, 10; Hearts: Ace, 9, 5; Diamonds: Queen, 10, 3; Clubs: Queen, Jack, 6, 4.
   What should you now bid as the opener?

QUIZ

1. Who chooses which pack of cards will be played with first?
2. What is the highest bid possible?
3. If the previous bid were 3 Diamonds and you want to bid Clubs: What is the lowest bid in Clubs that you can make?
4. What is the lowest bid possible?
5. If you pick up your hand and you have 2 Aces, 2 Kings and a Jack:
   (a) How many points do you have?
   (b) Can you open the bidding for your side?
6. A bid of 3 No Trumps contracts to make how many tricks?
7. How many high card points do you hold in Spades if you have A, J, 9, 5 and 4?
8. While your partner is dealing with one pack of cards
   (a) what are you doing? and
   (b) where do you put the second pack of cards?
9. When you make any bid can you suddenly raise your voice or make a face to show what you think of your cards?
10. Your partner has opened the bidding for your side and you have only one Ace in your hand and no other High Card Points.
    Can you reply?

3

Playing

After the bidding is over, the Declarer plays the hand and the opposition defend the hand. The person on the left of the Declarer plays the first card and puts it face up on the table.

Then the partner of the Declarer, called the 'Dummy', puts all his or her cards down on the table in suits facing the Declarer; if they are playing in a Trump Suit, that suit is put down on the left; if they are playing in No Trumps, the two red suits are placed in the middle. The dummy now takes no further part in this game – the Declarer playing both their cards.

After the first card has been played, the Declarer chooses a card from Dummy and puts it on top of the first one, the third card is played and then the Declarer's. The first card determines which suit is to be played by all four players in that particular trick.

The general rule throughout the game is that the 2nd player plays low, the 3rd player plays high, and the 4th player tries to play even higher. However, there are 5 Honour cards in each suit and there is another rule: cover an Honour with an Honour. So, if the player making the opening lead in any hand plays a Jack and you, as 2nd player, had the Queen, you would break the first rule, and play your Queen – hoping that this would mean that the opener's partner would have to play an even higher card, so that the trick was not won with a measly Jack. Nothing in bridge is simple – is it? Neither of these are unbreakable rules – you can, and should, use your own judgment about all your play.

If the opponent on the right has won the bidding, you are the first player to put down a card just before the dummy lays down her cards. Try to play a suit that has been bid by your partner and not a suit bid by your opponents. Or, if the game is in No Trumps, play the 4th highest card of your longest suit, e.g. if you hold K, 9, 6, 5, 4, play the 5. Throughout the game be aware of any suit that your partner leads – it may quite possibly mean that he would like you to lead it back to him.

Getting Trumps Out

In the 1930s, when Rubber Bridge was being played for vast sums of money, there was a saying "There's many a man sleeping on the embankment because he didn't get out his trumps"! This means that after the Trump suit has been decided, the Declarer's aim must be to extract the Trumps from both of the opponents' hands, so that they are not able suddenly to win tricks because of their shortages in the suit that has been led. As the Declarer should have 8 Trumps between him and Dummy, the 5 Trumps lurking in the hot, sticky hands of the opposition most often are split 3-2; although a 4-1 split or even 5-0 is possible.

The Man who wouldn't lead Trumps.

A trick is won by the highest card played – and you must always follow suit. If you have none of that suit in your hand, you can Trump it: remember, a 2 of Trumps will beat an Ace of another suit.

If you have none of the suit led in your hand and either you do not wish to Trump, or you do not hold any Trumps, you can 'throw away' any other card that you do not think will be useful in the future play.

If you are playing in No Trumps, you and your partner have decided that you do not have a particularly good suit between you and all your suits are fairly equally distributed. In other words, you do not have a suit which shouts to be the Trump one – this having been decided in your joint bidding.

The unit of play is called 'a Rubber'. This is won by the first side to win two games. A game is won by scoring 100 or more points below the line of the scorecard. Your aim is to score more points than your opponents.

You score points by:
a) bidding and making your contract
b) by defeating the opponents at their contract
c) by earning bonus points.

Points below the line are scored only by bidding and making your contract.

Points above the line are:
(1) 'overtricks' – that is when you scored more tricks than you contracted to make, or
(2) points you gain for defeating your opponents or,
(3) bonus points which are: Honour points, points for a slam, doubling, or making a rubber. None of these points above the line counts towards game, but are added up with points below the line at the end of the rubber.

4

Scoring

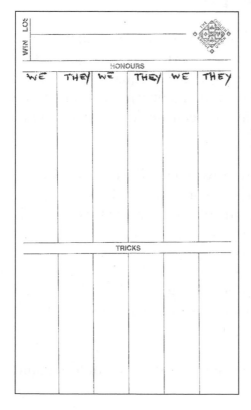

Bridge score card

You will see that a score card is generally divided into six vertical columns and bisected with a horizontal line. It is possible to score 3 rubbers in the six columns – two for each rubber, one for 'WE', you and your partner; and one for 'THEY', your two opponents. Every player at the table has their own scorecard, so that everyone is aware throughout the game of the current score.

No Trumps score 40 points for the first trick, that is the 1 over 6 and 30 for each one thereafter.

Spades	score 30 for each trick
Hearts	score 30 for each trick
Diamonds	score 20 for each trick
Clubs	score 20 for each trick

A game is 100 points or more. Therefore, winning with a contract of 3 No Trumps is game. A contract of 4 Spades or Hearts = 120 points – 3 Spades or Hearts would only equal 90 points and would not be enough for game. A contract of 5 Diamonds or Clubs = 100 points and is game.

Spades and Hearts are called the 'Major' suits, Diamonds and Clubs are called the 'Minor' suits.

'Non-Vulnerable' – means a game has not yet been scored by a partnership.

'Vulnerable' – means a game has been scored.

Below the horizontal line are points contracted and made. Therefore, if you bid 3 Hearts and made 9 tricks, you would score 3 x 30 points below the line. If you made 10 tricks, the extra trick that you had not 'contracted' to make, would be placed above the line. The point of using a scorecard is to see how you and your partner are progressing throughout a game. There is nothing more irritating than to bid 3 Hearts (equalling 90 points) when you already have 60 points below the line, and only needed to bid '2 Hearts' (another 60 points) to make a game, and then you, disastrously, only make 8 tricks!

Two games won outright, a Rubber, for one partnership scores 700 points above the line; if three games are necessary the first side to win 2 games scores 500 points.

If 5 Diamonds is bid and declarer (the person playing the hand) only makes nine tricks, he has failed to make his contract by two tricks – therefore he has lost and his opponents get some points:

a) 50 points above the line, for each trick down, irrespective of which suit or No Trumps has been played, when declarer is non-vulnerable;
b) 100 points above the line, for each trick down when declarer is vulnerable.

Therefore, in the example of the 5 Diamonds bid (11 tricks) and only 9 tricks made, the opponents would score 100 points if declarer were non-vulnerable, and 200 points if declarer were vulnerable.

Points below the line are called a 'part-score' and can be added to your other part-score or scores in the next game(s). However, once one partnership has succeeded in making at least 100 points below the line, a game, their opponents' score below the line only counts as if it were above the line – it is no longer counting towards their game and both sides start again from zero for the next game.

Honours.   HASSALL

Honours
Any 4 of the top 5 cards, not necessarily consecutive, in one hand of the suit that are Trumps, score 100 points above the line; all 5, score 150. All 4 Aces in one hand, in a No Trump contract, score 150 points above the line. Honours must be declared at the end of the game and before the first card of the next game is dealt. There are people who, when they first pick up their hand, and when

the suit has been decided for the game, will announce their Honours there and then; this may, no doubt, give incredible pleasure to their partner, but, it also gives far too much information to their opponents.

QUIZ

1. Which suits are the minors?
2. Must you trump if you cannot follow suit?
3. Which is the lowest ranking suit?
4. Which counts more in scoring hearts or spades?
5. What is a part-score? and can you combine two or more to make a game?
6. What scores above the line?
7. You score 60 below the line and in the next game you score another 60 below the line.
   How much can you carry forward to the subsequent game?
8. If you and your partner contract to make 3 Diamonds and make 4, what do you score?
9. Can you refuse to follow suit even if you can do so?
10. How many cards can each player see, after the first card has been played?

SCORING EXERCISE

Both N/S and E/W are non-vulnerable, as it is the start of a game. If possible, put the scores for N/S and E/W on a score sheet.

1. N/S bid 5 Diamonds and made 8 tricks   (Non-vulnerable)
2. E/W bid 3 No Trumps and made 10 tricks   (Non-vulnerable)
3. N/S bid 4 Spades and made 9 tricks   (Non-vulnerable)
4. N/S bid 5 Clubs and made 7 tricks   (Non-vulnerable)
5. E/W bid 4 Hearts and made 8 tricks   (Vulnerable)
6. N/S bid 4 Spades and made 12 tricks   (Non-vulnerable)
7. N/S bid 2 Hearts and made 9 tricks   (Vulnerable)
8. E/W bid 4 Diamonds and made 6 Tricks   (Vulnerable)
9. E/W bid 1 Club and made 5 tricks   (Vulnerable)
10. N/S bid 5 Diamonds and made 12 tricks   (Vulnerable)

5

Maths

Bridge is a game which needs simple maths. The main point to remember is that there are 40 High Card Points (HCP) in every pack of cards. If your partner opens, she will have a minimum of 12 points and if you reply you have a minimum of 6 points; therefore the least you can have together is 18 points which leaves the opponents with 22 points. In your bidding 'conversation' you are trying to tell your partner if you have more points than this and, if appropriate, so is she.

To BID AND WIN GAME in No Trumps (9 tricks), Hearts and Spades (10 tricks) you need to have 25-26 points between you. To bid and win game in Diamonds and Clubs (11 tricks) you need to have 29 points between you. These are, of course, rough estimates, as the distribution of cards can create variations.

FOR A LITTLE SLAM (bidding 6 tricks, and thus winning 12 tricks) you need at least 32 points (preferably 34) between you.

FOR A GRAND SLAM (winning all the 13 tricks available) you need 34+ points (preferably 37) between you. The point about bidding for a Slam is that you get an enormous amount of extra points above the line – more about that in another lesson.

WHICH SUIT TO BID. Provided you have enough points to open for your partnership you should choose your longest suit – it is the length of the suit, not its High Card Points, that determines your best suit. You could open with a 4 card suit, if No Trumps were not appropriate, but a 5 card suit is infinitely preferable. If your partner opens with 1 Heart and then re-bids the Hearts, she has 5 Hearts; if she then bids it for the third time, she has 6 Hearts.

You can, therefore, work out whether you can support her in the suit she has bid if you are certain you have that all-important 8 Trumps between you, which leaves only 5 Trumps in your opponents' hands.

To support your partner after the first bid you must have 4 of that suit; after the second bid of her same suit, you only need 3; and with the third bid of that suit, 2 will make up your requisite 8 trumps.

The opener with both a 5 card suit and a 4 card suit should bid the 5 card suit first, then the 4 card one, followed by the 5 card one again. If you have bid a suit and your partner has not supported you in that suit, give her another suit with at least 4 cards in it, which she might prefer.

OVERCALLING. If your opponents have opened the bidding for their side, you can make a bid with less than the required 12 points, provided you have a 5 card suit, or better, and at least 8 points (preferably 10). But be very careful, because your partner will not know whether you have only these 8 points or a good opening hand.

NO TRUMPS. As you only need 9 tricks (bidding 3) to get a game (40 + 30 + 30 points), a No Trump call is a good contract. But there are dangers. If, between you, you do not have 'cover' – that is, the ability to win tricks at least once, preferably twice, in any particular suit – then your opponents could march onwards with that suit, if it were a long one, as there are no Trumps to block them.

No Trumps.　　　Hassall

If you do not have a 5 card suit and have 12-14 points, it is a good idea to open 1 No Trump. But be careful if you only have a singleton (that is, one card in a suit) or even a doubleton (2 cards in a suit), unless they are nice high ones, or your partner has bid that suit. Only bid 1 No Trump at the start of the bidding, if the opponents have already opened the bidding; you cannot overcall 1 No Trump. (I will explain this later.)

To respond to your partner's opening bid with a 'No Trump' is very useful and keeps the bidding open for him or her. Remember, if there have been three 'No Bids', then your partner cannot make another bid. If your partner has opened the bidding with 1 of a suit, you know that she has at least 12 points and that she would like the suit she has mentioned to be trumps.

Supposing that the opposition do not bid, your partner would not have another chance to bid and either mention the same or another suit. If you have 6-9 points, without 4 cards of your partner's bid suit, and no 4 or 5 card suit of your own, nor a singleton, you should reply 1 No Trump, thus keeping the bidding open, telling your partner what you have and giving him or her the chance to choose the suit he or she wishes to select.

QUIZ

1. Your partner has opened the bidding with 1 Heart. You reply 1 No Trump and she then re-bids 2 Hearts.
   What does she have in her hand?
2. Why is it easier to bid and get a game in No Trumps?
3. What are the pitfalls in bidding No Trumps?
4. You bid 1 No Trump – there are no more bids and you make 2 No Trumps.
   What do you score?
5. You have 12 points and 2 Hearts, 4 Spades, 4 Diamonds and 3 Clubs.
   (a) Can you open with No Trumps?
   (b) Which suit should you look at most carefully?
6. You have bid and made 3 Diamonds.
   (a) What do you now need to get a game?
   (b) Would 1 Heart do it?, or 1 No Trump?, or 2 Clubs?
7. You have A, K, Q, 10 of Hearts in your hand.
   (a) How many points is that?
   (b) Do you score anything if that suit is trumps?
8. You have worked out that you and your partner have fairly good hands, but one of the opponents has made a bid which was not an overcall, and their partner has replied 1 No Trump.
   (a) What is the maximum number of points that your partnership can hold?
   (b) Can you bid to a game?
9. You have bid 1 Heart, your partner has replied 1 Spade. You have 14 points but hate Spades having only two little ones, so you re-bid 2 Hearts, having 5 of them (not just 4). She obviously loathes your Hearts, but offers another suit by saying 3 Clubs. You have 4 nice Diamonds.
   What should you call now?
10. You call 3 No Trumps but make only 7 tricks – you are vulnerable.
    How many points do you give away?

6

The Weakness Take-Out

Now this is a 'convention' – a very easy one, but necessary (sorry!).

You are learning a form of Acol bridge, which means that you are using the 'Weak No Trump', requiring an opening bid of 12-14 points. Now you are going to learn a response to it.

If your partner has the right number of points, even distribution, no 5 card major suit and no singletons, she will open a No Trump. If you hold 0-10 points and a 5 card or longer suit (this is most important) you bid 2 of that suit.

The point of this so-called 'weakness take-out' is that it is probably easier to get your contract in a suit, even if it is at the 2 level, as you will, hopefully, have at least 8 trumps between you (the 1 No Trump opener must have at least 2 of your 5 card suit). Whereas trying to get 1 No Trump with very few points between you could be terribly difficult.

The first bidder who has called the No Trump must say No Bid the second time round, if his or her partner has done the weakness take-out.

So the sequence will be: First: '1 No Trump'; Partner replies: '2 Hearts', meaning that she has under 11 points and 5 Hearts. The first bidder knows that the most she and her partner can have between them is $14 + 10 = 24$, and the least they could have between them is $12 + 0 = 12$, so she now says 'No bid'.

If, after your partner has opened 1 No Trump, you do not
have a 5 card suit, and have under 11 points, you must say
No Bid.

Example 1   Weakness Take-Out
North deals

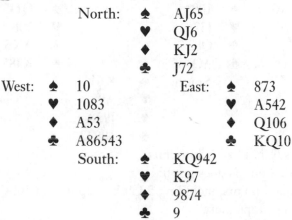

	North:	♠	AJ65
		♥	QJ6
		♦	KJ2
		♣	J72

West:	♠	10	East:	♠	873
	♥	1083		♥	A542
	♦	A53		♦	Q106
	♣	A86543		♣	KQ10

	South:	♠	KQ942
		♥	K97
		♦	9874
		♣	9

North has 13 points and even distribution, therefore opens '1 NT'.
East has 11 points, even distribution and cannot overcall 1 NT, so
says 'No Bid'.
South has 8 points, and 5 Spades, so replies '2 Spades'.
West says 'No Bid'.
North ends the bidding by also saying 'No Bid'.
The Contract is therefore 2 Spades.

I would suggest laying out all the cards and first playing it as if South
had not replied to his partner, so North was playing 1 No Trump.
Then lay them out again and try the contract as 2 Spades – you will
see that Clubs in the second example could be lethal!

Example 2   Weakness Take–Out
East deals

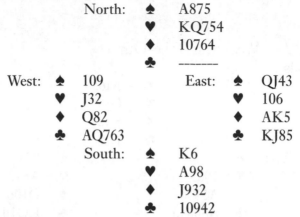

North: ♠ A875
        ♥ KQ754
        ♦ 10764
        ♣ ---------

West: ♠ 109   East: ♠ QJ43
       ♥ J32   ♥ 106
       ♦ Q82   ♦ AK5
       ♣ AQ763   ♣ KJ85

        South: ♠ K6
                ♥ A98
                ♦ J932
                ♣ 10942

East opens '1 NT' with 14 points.
South with 8 points does not bid.
West having 9 points, including 5 Clubs, replies '2 Clubs'.
The bidding stops there.
In No Trumps, Hearts would have been a great problem for East and West.

QUIZ

1. You have seven points, 5 Clubs and your partner has opened 1 No Trump.
   What do you bid?
2. You have 8 points and no five card suit and your partner has opened 1 No Trump.
   What do you bid?

7
Revision

At last you can relax and not have to learn anything new for a bit!

First, each player selects one card from the pack which is laid out face down, in a fan shape, on the table. Generally the players picking the two higher cards play together, and the players with the two lower cards play together.

The highest card (nearest the Ace of Spades) is the winner and can choose where to sit and which cards they wish to play with. The chosen pack is passed to the left and shuffled, and then passed over to the right and cut – the 'winner' then deals out all the cards, starting with the person on the left. Meanwhile, the other pack is being shuffled by the dealer's partner and is then placed on their right, so that next time the prospective dealer can pick up that pack and pass it across so that it is cut by the person on their left – "If you're not a fool quite, put the cards on your right", or "if, of your wits, you are quite bereft, put your cards upon the left"!

There are 13 cards in each hand – sort them into suits and count your High Card Points (4 for an Ace, 3 for a King, 2 for a Queen, 1 for a Jack). There are, therefore, 40 HCP in a pack. You need a minimum of 12 HCP to open the bidding for your side, and your partner needs a minimum of 6 HCP to reply.

The aim of Bridge is to win a Rubber. A Rubber is the first of the two pairs to win two games (so a Rubber could be either two clear games, or three – with one side winning two, and one winning only one). A rubber scores 500 points above the line if three games have been necessary, and 700 if one side has won with two clear games. A game is at least 100 points below the line. Below the line are points that you have contracted to make – any extra tricks go above the line and do not count towards game (although they are added in at the end). Part scores can be added to in other games.

The ranking order of the cards is No Trumps, Spades, Hearts, Diamonds and Clubs. No Trumps scores 40 for the first trick and 30 for each subsequent trick (therefore you need to bid 3 NT for a game); Spades and Hearts score 30 for each trick (so you need to bid 4 for a game); and Diamonds and Clubs score 20 for each trick (so you need to bid 5 for a game). Please note that although you have to win the first six tricks, when you bid you ignore them – so 2 Hearts means a Contract to win 6 + 2 tricks which equals 8.

To bid a game in No Trumps, Hearts or Spades you need between you 25–26 points, and to bid a game in Diamonds and Clubs you need between you 29 points.

A trick is won by the highest card played on it (or, if someone cannot follow suit, because he or she does not have any of that particular suit, by trumping it).

The point of bidding is to have a conversation with your partner – the aim is to have 8 trumps between you (so there are only 5 out against you). When you open the bidding it is vastly preferable to have 5 of one suit, although you can bid with only 4, and then you try to find out if your partner approves of that suit. If you have only 4 in a suit, you do not bid it again, but with 5 in a suit, you can re-bid it.

The bidding stops when there have been three No Bids. Bidding progresses upwards: 1 Club, 1 Diamond, 1 Heart, 1 Spade, 1 No Trump, 2 Clubs, 2 Diamonds, etc. Of course, not everything is mentioned. The first of the partnership who has mentioned the suit (or No Trumps) wins the right to play the hand and their partner is the Dummy and lays down their cards on the table, after the person sitting on the declarer's left plays the first card. Dummy takes no further part in that particular hand.

If you have an even hand – no five card major suits, no single cards – you can bid 1 No Trump, but you must have between 12 and 14 points only. Your partner can reply with 0–10 points as long as they hold a 5 card suit because it is easier to bid and win with a Trump contract than it is to play No Trumps with very few points between you. This is called the 'weakness take-out'.

If your partner has opened the bidding with 1 of a suit all you know is that there are at least 4 cards in that suit and 12 points. Of course, it may be much stronger. If you have between 6 and 9 points, no good 4 or 5 card suit of your own, and no singletons, you can bid 1 NT just to keep the bidding open for your partner, in case they might want to go higher. If the opponent before you does bid, you need not reply if you are weak, because your partner will have another chance to bid again.

Points above the line are scored if the other side do not win their contract – 50 points for each trick are scored by the opponents if the contracted side is not vulnerable (that is, has not already won one game) and 100 points for each trick if they are vulnerable.

Extra tricks that have been won over and above the contracted number are scored at their face value (30 for No Trumps, Spades and Hearts and 20 for Diamonds and Clubs).

Bonus points are scored for holding Honours (any 4 of the Ace, King, Queen, Jack, Ten) in any one hand if that is the Trump suit, scores 100, and all 5 Honours score 150. If you are playing in No Trumps and hold all 4 Aces in one hand you score 150. These points are all scored above the line and must be claimed at the end of that game and before the first card of the next game has been dealt.

QUIZ

1. Your partner bids 1NT and you have no points and 5 Hearts. What do you bid?
2. You have 14 points and 5 Hearts and bid 1 Heart. Your partner replies 2 Hearts. What do you think this means?
3. You have scored 70 points below the line. What did you contract to make?
4. You have scored 60 below the line and 30 above. What was your contracted bid?
5. You have won a Rubber outright (the other side have not won a game). What do you score, and where do you put it on the score sheet?
6. You and your partner obviously like Diamonds, but you have only 7 points. Do you try to go for a game in Diamonds?
7. You have 15 points and 5 Hearts and your partner has replied 1 No Trump. What do you bid on the second round?
8. Your opponents bid 4 Spades and only made 8 tricks, but they have already made a game. How much do you score and where do you put it on the scorecard?

8

Revision again,
and Overcalling with a No Trump

Re-iteration is the spice of life – are you now completely relaxed?

We need to revise some essential numbers:

There are 40 High Card Points in a pack (Ace = 4, King = 3, Queen = 2, Jack = 1).

You need at least 12 points to open the bidding for your side, unless the opponent has bid first, in which case you might open with only 8–10 points, and a 5 card suit; this is called an 'overcall' – but be careful.

You need at least 6 points to reply.

Remember, bidding is a conversation between partners – you are trying to give the right information to your partner.

To win a game (100 or more below the line) – you need 29 points between you for the minor suits (Clubs and Diamonds); 25/26 points for the Major Suits (Hearts and Spades); and 25/26 for No Trumps.

To open 1 No Trump you need 12-14 points and even distribution of suits – no five card major suit and no singletons.

To reply to 1 No Trump – if you have a five card suit and under 11 points – bid 2 of that suit; the opener should then say No Bid.

To play in a Trump contract you should have at least 8 cards between you in that suit.

If your partner has been the first bidder and has opened 1 of a suit you know he or she must have 4 of that suit and at least 12 points; you should only support him or her in that suit if you have 4 of the same suit on your first response, so that you have 8 Trumps between you. If she had 5 of the suit, she would re-bid them and you, as the partner, could support with only 3 of that suit.

If your partner has opened the bidding with 1 of a suit and you have an even hand and 6-9 points, reply 1 No Trump in order to keep it open for her to re-bid if she wishes.

NOW FOR SOME NEW INFORMATION!

Overcalling With A No Trump
If you have 15-19 points and possibly even distribution (although you could have a 5 card suit, say, 5,3,3,2, although the 5 card suit must not be a major suit) open 1 of your best suit even if it is a 4 card suit because you cannot bid 1 No Trump since you have more than 12 14 points.

On your second bid say No Trumps; this shows at least 15 points and your partner can add your combined points together and decide what to do. If possible, with 15-16 points, just bid 1 No Trump; with 17/18 points jump to 2 No Trumps, with 19 points jump to 3 No Trumps.

If your opponent bids 1 NT or 1 of a suit before you, and you have 15-19 points and fairly even distribution, you can overcall with a NT bid, although you could not have made this bid if you had been the first opening bidder.

So – you hold 18 points: Spades A, K, 4; Hearts K, J, 9, 2; Diamonds A, 3, 2; Clubs Q, J, 8 = 18 points. You open 1 Heart; your partner replies 1 Spade; you re-bid 2 No Trumps. As your partner knows that he holds 10 points in his own hand and that you must have at least 17 or 18 points, he realizes that, as he has 4 Hearts in his own hand and knows that you, too, must have 4 Hearts in your hand, there are enough points and trumps for a game in Hearts, so he will jump to 4 Hearts.

Because of this information there is a point I would like to make about opening with 12-14 points and a 5 card minor suit and 5, 3, 3, 2 distribution. It is better to bid 1 No Trump and then on your second bid call the five card suit, because otherwise if you bid the minor suit first you could not continue with a No Trump without your partner thinking that you had over 15 points.

One Up – Shut Up
If you bid 1 of a suit and your partner replies with the same suit at the 2 level, it implies that she has four of that suit, but only 6–9 points. The opening bidder should respond No Bid.

4 Card and 5 Card Suits
Strict Acol Bridge says that with 'two equal ranking suits you should always open the higher, whether they be 4 or 5 cards in each suit', and you may well decide to do this later when you are established players.

However, there are different views on this, and I consider that giving a little more information to your partner as to whether you have a 4 or 5 card suit could be useful:

With two 4 card suits, bid the <u>lower</u> value suit first. Although, some pundits say that if you hold 4 Hearts and 4 Spades you are supposed to bid the higher ranking suit. I am inclined to think that this could be very muddling, so I ignore it!

With two 5 card suits, bid the <u>higher</u> value suit first.

Officially, if you hold a singleton card and three 4 card suits, and 12 or more points, you should bid the suit immediately below the singleton, if it were a red singleton; (R.S.B., which means Red Singleton Below); and the middle of the 4 card suits if it were a black singleton (B.S.M., which means Black Singleton Middle). However, it is probably much simpler to bid your lowest 4 card suit and continue with the next higher ranking, hoping that you and your partner will find some agreement.

Responding To Your Partner
If your partner has opened it is better to bid your own 5 card suit, but you can reply with your 4 card suit if you do not hold a 5 card suit. And, of course, you can support partner with four of her bid suit.

Example 1   Overcalling a No Trump
West deals

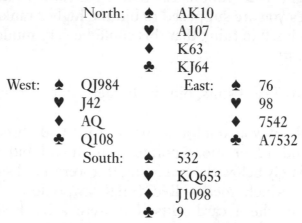

North: ♠ AK10
            ♥ A107
            ♦ K63
            ♣ KJ64

West: ♠ QJ984   East: ♠ 76
       ♥ J42   ♥ 98
       ♦ AQ   ♦ 7542
       ♣ Q108   ♣ A7532

South: ♠ 532
             ♥ KQ653
             ♦ J1098
             ♣ 9

West has 12 points and 5 Spades, so opens '1 Spade'.

North has 18 points and even distribution, so bids '2 No Trumps', alerting his partner to his number of points and showing that he has good Spades (the opposition's suit).

East says 'No Bid'.

South has 5 Hearts and 6 points, so bids '3 Hearts', the weakness take-out.

North, with 3 of his partner's Hearts, calls '4 Hearts'.

South says 'No Bid'.

Example 2   Overcalling a No Trump
East deals

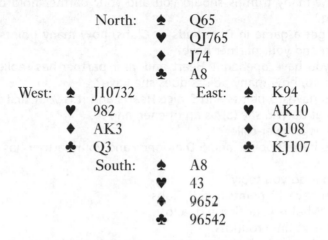

North: ♠   Q65
         ♥   QJ765
         ♦   J74
         ♣   A8

West: ♠ J10732   East: ♠ K94
       ♥ 982   ♥ AK10
       ♦ AK3   ♦ Q108
       ♣ Q3   ♣ KJ107

South: ♠   A8
         ♥   43
         ♦   9652
         ♣   96542

East has a No Trump shape, but has too many points to open a No Trump, therefore, she bids her 4 card suit, saying '1 Club'.
South says 'No Bid'.
West responds to her partner with '1 Spade'.
North passes.
East then bids '1 No Trump', meaning she has 15/16 points.
West, with 10 points, knowing that her partner holds a minimum of 15 points and that, therefore, with her own points they should have enough for a game in a major suit, does a jump bid to '3 Spades'. She does not bid a game, because she is not sure whether her opening partner likes Spades.
East, encouraged by her partner's jump bid, knowing her partner must have at least 5 Spades as she has bid them twice, and holding 3 Spades, bids '4 Spades'.

REVISION QUIZ

1. How many trumps should you and your partner hold between you?
2. To get a game in Diamonds or Clubs, how many points should you and your partner have?
3. If you have opened 1 Heart and your partner has replied a No Trump, how many points does she have?
4. You have 10 points and 5 nice Hearts and it is your first bid. What do you say (a) as an opener, and
   (b) as an over-caller?
5. You have 2 points and 5 Diamonds and your partner has opened 1 NT.
   What do you reply?
6. You have 17 points and 5 Clubs.
   (a) What is your first bid, and
   (b) next time round?
7. You have bid 5 Diamonds and are vulnerable, and have only scored 8 tricks.
   What is the score?
8. What does 'one-up, shut-up' mean in the context of bidding?
9. You have 18 points: Spades J654; Hearts AKQ; Diamonds KQ10; Clubs QJ2.
   What do you bid?
   (a) As the opener, and,
   (b) as an overcall, if your opponent has bid?
10. Your partner has bid Hearts and the opponents have won the bidding (they are playing in Clubs).
    It is your lead, which card do you play?

9

The Losing Trick Count

You have learnt to assess your hand by counting your High Card Points (HCP). There are 3 other methods that some may use:

a) Quick Tricks – this used to be very popular, but is now regarded as rather old fashioned. If you hold A, K, in a suit, that would be 2 Quick Tricks, because you are almost certain to win with both of them and the A, Q, would be $1\frac{1}{2}$ Quick Tricks. I am just telling you this because sometimes you may hear someone talking about them.

b) Sometimes, once the trumps have been agreed, people add extra points either for length (counting 1 extra point for any suit with 5 cards in it, 2 points for 6 cards, etc.); or shortage points (counting 3 for a void, 2 for a singleton, and 1 for a doubleton).

c) A third method is using something called the 'Losing Trick Count', in conjunction with your HCP, which is, I consider, an infinitely superior method. There are some players who will insist that this Losing Trick Count only really works once Trumps have been decided. Personally, I start using it as soon as I pick up my hand and although it is not infallible, it is amazing how many times it is successful.

When you have picked up your hand and sorted it into suits (separating the red and black suits, so as not to get muddled), you will add the HCP you hold. As soon as you have counted the HCP, you must start another count.

If you have 3 or more cards in any suit, and these are not the Ace, King and Queen, they will be Losers. If you hold only one card, unless it is the Ace, it is a Loser. Two cards in a suit must be the Ace and King. You can never have more than 3 losers in any one suit, however many cards may be in that suit, as you only count the first three. A void in a suit counts as no Losers.

To open the bidding you need 7 or fewer Losers in your hand; to reply, you need 9 or fewer.

So, if your partner opens the bidding, you *presume* she has 7 Losers. If the responder replies, you *presume* she has 9 Losers. If either have fewer, it is treated as if they had a much better hand.

Of course, you need a good Trump fit so that you and your partner have at least 8 cards in one suit.

Examples:
a) If you hold Hearts A, K, 9, 4, 3, Spades K, 3, Diamonds, 7, 6, 5, 4, 3, Clubs 8, your HCP are 10; *but,* your losers are: Hearts 1, Spades 1, Diamonds 3, Clubs 1. You have therefore only 6 losers and can certainly overcall your opponent with a Heart.

   If your partner then replied, you would give her the benefit of the doubt, and presume that she has 9 or fewer Losers. Therefore, your 6, and her 9 = 15 potential Losing Tricks; and subtracting 15 from 18 means you can bid 3 of a suit (the 'Rule of 18').

b) You can use the Losing Trick Count in a more flexible way. Suppose you open 1 Heart, and your partner replies 2 Clubs, and you don't like Clubs, but have 5 Hearts, you would re-bid 2 Hearts; your partner has 3 Hearts and only 8 Losers, and so bids 3 Hearts, and you realise that she must have only 8 Losers as she has bid 3 (presuming that you had 7 Losers); but, as you only have 6 Losers (not 7), you triumphantly bid for game with 4 Hearts ($8+6 = 14$; $18-14 = 4$).

However, the Losing Trick Count does not work with No Trumps, since it is based on unequal distribution, and not the No Trump even distribution. You may find that you are equally good in all the suits and have 12–14 points, but your 'Losers' could be as many as 9 instead of the 7 you need to open in a suit contract. However you could still open with a No Trump, and your partner will know that you could have 7, 8, or 9 Losers.

Remember – *Nothing In Bridge Is Written In Stone* – and that is the fun of bridge. These are guidelines, but you really should not be bidding for your partnership in a suit contract with more than 7 losers, as your partner needs to know that this is definite.

Losing Trick Count – Why the number 18?
Each of the partners could have a maximum of 12 Losing Tricks (that is three cards in all four suits not having either an Ace, King or Queen). Therefore there could be 24 Losing Tricks between them.

Deduct the actual numbers of Losers that you and your partner have from this figure of 24 – and that is the number of tricks you can hopefully make.

For example, you have 7 Losers and your partner has continued to bid up to the 3 level, so you *presume* that she has 8 Losers: $7 + 8 = 15$, $24 - 15 = 9$; so you should be able to make 9 tricks. We, of course, count this as 3 tricks not 9, because of those 6 tricks which always have to be made before you can start counting; when you bid 1 H you have to make $6 + 1$ tricks and therefore we take that 6 from the 24 and arrive at that magic number – 18!

QUIZ

How many Losers do each of these hands hold?

1. Spades 6; Hearts A, K, 3; Diamonds Q, 8, 6, 4, 2; Clubs A, 4, 3, 2.
2. Spades J, 10, 9, 7, 3; Hearts Q, J, 10; Diamonds A; Clubs Q, J, 9, 8.
3. Spades none; Hearts 9, 8, 7, 6, 5, 4, 2; Diamonds K, 3; Clubs K, 7, 6, 5.
4. Spades A, K, Q, 8, 5, 4, 2; Hearts none; Diamonds J, 10, 9, 7, 5; Clubs 10.

You will see that distribution works wonders. For example, in No. 3, where there are only 6 points but the losers are very low; and in No. 4 where the long suit and the void make it a very strong hand.

It would be a good idea to deal out several hands and work out for yourself how many losers there are in each hand.

10

Strong Weakness Take-Out

You have learned about the weakness take-out, which is after your partner opens 1 No Trump and you have 0-10 points, and a 5 card suit. Now, supposing, in response to that 1 No Trump bid you have more than 10 points? What do you do? Very simple. You jump in that 5 card suit. So, if you have 13 points, for example, you know that your opening partner has at least 12 points, so you are within sight of a game in a major suit.

The bidding would, therefore, be:

Opener: 1 No Trump
Partner: 3 Hearts (I have at least 5 Hearts and at least 11 Points)

Opener can then decide what she wishes to do, depending on whether she has 12, 13, or 14 points, and, if she has at least 3 of your Hearts, she may put you up in that suit. If the responding partner has at least 11 points and 6 Hearts, she should immediately jump to 4 Hearts.

If, after your partner's opening bid of that 1 No Trump, you say No bid, she will know that you have no 5 card suit, even distribution and 0-9 points. If you reply 2 No Trumps it means that you have even distribution and hold 10-12 points. And a reply of 3 No Trumps means that you have 13-18 points. None of these No Trump replies mean that you are adamant about playing in No Trumps, it is merely giving the amount of points you hold.

Example 1   **Strong weakness take-out**
East deals

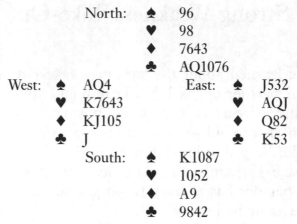

North: ♠   96
         ♥   98
         ♦   7643
         ♣   AQ1076

West: ♠   AQ4   East: ♠   J532
        ♥   K7643   ♥   AQJ
        ♦   KJ105   ♦   Q82
        ♣   J   ♣   K53

South: ♠   K1087
         ♥   1052
         ♦   A9
         ♣   9842

East with 13 points and even distribution opens '1 No Trump' (she has 8 losers, but the Losing Trick count does not work with No Trumps).

South passes.

West has 14 points (and 6 losers), so she jumps in her 5 card suit to '4 Hearts', knowing they have a minimum of 12 + 14 = 26 points between them, and East must have at least 2 Hearts.

In No Trumps, East/West would have lost 4 Clubs, 1 Diamond, and maybe 1 Spade.

Example 2   Strong weakness take-out
South deals

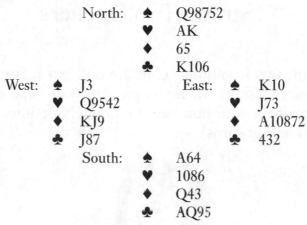

North: ♠   Q98752
        ♥   AK
        ♦   65
        ♣   K106

West: ♠   J3   East: ♠   K10
      ♥   Q9542   ♥   J73
      ♦   KJ9   ♦   A10872
      ♣   J87   ♣   432

South: ♠   A64
       ♥   1086
       ♦   Q43
       ♣   AQ95

South opens '1 No trump'.

West says 'No Bid' as she has 9 losers.

North, with 12 points a 6 card suit and only 6 losers, responds to his partner, '4 Spades', as he fears that South might well not bid up to a game.

East, South and West say 'No Bid'.

It might be a good idea to deal out both these examples and try playing them first in No Trumps, and then in the suit contracts. This should make it apparent how well the weakness take-out works.

11

Strong Two Openers

All right, this is another 'contraption', but it is necessary for those occasions when you pick up your hand and gasp with delight at your number of points. Sometimes they are called 'Forcing Twos'.

Forcing.

If you have 20-22 points and no 5 card suit and even distribution (important because you can be left in it), open 2 No Trumps; your partner does *not* have to reply, but should give her 5 card suit, or she could put you up into 3 No Trumps with as little as 4 points and even distribution.

When you hold 19-22 points and, hopefully, 4 or fewer Losing Tricks, and a 4 or 5 card suit, you open with 2 of that suit, then your partner *must* reply unless there has been an intervening bid. If she has nothing (i.e. under 4 points), she will say 2 No Trumps to keep the bidding open. Otherwise, with more points, she will bid her best suit or support you in your suit.

The aim of the Strong Two Opening bid is to tell your partner your strength and see if a Slam is possible. First you must decide which suit (or No Trumps) is the best. If you think that you may be able to make 12 or even 13 tricks, you need to have 32+ points, preferably 34, between you for a Small Slam; and 37 for a Grand Slam. But always remember to count your Losing Tricks because you could call and make a Slam with many fewer points than these because of the distribution – I have bid and made a Grand Slam with only 11 points between my partner and myself but with a very low number of Losing Tricks.

However, you must obviously find out if, between you, you hold the Aces and Kings, which are really necessary, if you are hoping to lose none or one trick at the most.

It is very important to have decided exactly what you wish to be your final suit or No Trumps before you start asking about the Aces and Kings.

The simplest way to ask, in my opinion, is the *Blackwood Convention* which will ascertain whether your partner is holding the Aces and/or Kings that you need to bid your contract. To use Blackwood you bid 4 No Trumps which, as 3 No Trumps is a game, is only kept for this convention.

The responses are:

5 Clubs meaning 0 or 4 Aces (although it is highly unlikely that you would be calling for Aces if you held none yourself!)

5 Diamonds meaning 1 Ace
5 Hearts   meaning 2 Aces
5 Spades   meaning 3 Aces

If the person who is asking finds that her partner holds the required number of Aces, she continues the bidding by saying 5 No Trumps. Or, perhaps they are missing one ace, but she hopes that they will have all the Kings between them. The responses are:

6 Clubs =	0 or 4 Kings
6 Diamonds =	1 King
6 Hearts =	2 Kings
6 Spades =	3 Kings

So, be aware that if your partner bids 4 No Trumps, it means she is trying for a slam in the last suit that has been mentioned by you.

The bidding may have gone:

You:	2 Hearts	Partner:	2 Spades
You:	3 Diamonds	Partner:	3 Hearts
			(I prefer Hearts to Diamonds)
You:	4 No Trumps	Partner:	5 Diamonds
			(1 Ace)
You:	5 No Trumps	Partner:	6 Diamonds
You:	6 Hearts		(1 King)

From this exchange your partner (and your opponents) will know that you have 19-22 points, 5 Hearts and, probably, only 4 Diamonds. Also they know that when you bid 4 No Trumps you were agreeing the last bid of Hearts made by your partner, and that you are trying for a Slam in that suit. She replies with 1 Ace and because you have at least 2, probably 3, yourself, you do not withdraw into 5 Hearts, but continue by asking for your partner's Kings, by calling 5 No Trumps. Whatever the response, you are prepared to bid 6 Hearts – a Small Slam.

The snag with Blackwood is that you may get too high too fast and find out that you are missing very necessary Kings without which you may be unable to make your contract. So, *be careful*. If your decided suits are Hearts, Spades or

No Trumps you have some leeway, but if you are in Diamonds or Clubs you could come unstuck.

Say you want to bid a Slam in Clubs. You have found out that you have all 4 Aces between you, and you ask for Kings by saying 5 No Trumps (you have 2 Kings yourself); your partner replies 6 Diamonds = 1 King. You are missing a King, so will probably not be able to make a grand Slam and you are now unable to bid Clubs except by saying 7 Clubs. Horrid!

Example 1   Strong Two openers
South deals

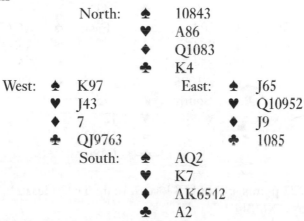

	North:	♠	10843
		♥	A86
		♦	Q1083
		♣	K4
West: ♠ K97			East: ♠ J65
♥ J43			♥ Q10952
♦ 7			♦ J9
♣ QJ9763			♣ 1085
	South:	♠	AQ2
		♥	K7
		♦	AK6542
		♣	A2

South is thrilled to pick up a hand and find 20 points and only 4 losers. He opens his best suit by bidding '2 Diamonds'.
West has only 7 points and says 'No Bid'.
North, having 9 points, gives a positive response and replies '3 Diamonds', supporting his partner.
East says 'No Bid'.
South needs to find out whether his partner has that missing Ace, so bids '4 No Trumps'.
North responds '5 Diamond' (i.e. 1 Ace).

South now realises that they have all the Aces, but there are still 2 Kings out against him. He bids '5 No Trumps', because if the reply were to be '6 Hearts' (i.e. 2 Kings), they will have all the Aces and all the Kings and he will be quite happy to go to '7 Diamonds'. On the other hand, if his partner replies '6 Diamonds', he will leave it as a Small Slam in Diamonds, knowing that the opponents have the one missing King.

Example 2 Strong Two Opener
East deals

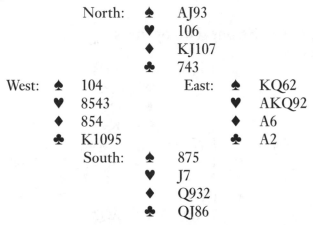

	North: ♠ AJ93	
	♥ 106	
	♦ KJ107	
	♣ 743	
West: ♠ 104		East: ♠ KQ62
♥ 8543		♥ AKQ92
♦ 854		♦ A6
♣ K1095		♣ A2
	South: ♠ 875	
	♥ J7	
	♦ Q932	
	♣ QJ86	

East has 22 points and only 3 losers, so opens '2 Hearts'.

South says 'No Bid'.

West has only 3 points, and 10 losers, and responds '2 No Trumps' (indicating she has a poor hand).

North says 'No Bid'.

East is disappointed, but bids '3 Spades' to indicate she has a 4 card suit as well, in case West might like Spades.

But, West, having told her opening partner that she has very few points, bids '4 Hearts' to show she prefers that suit. The bidding stops there.

Example 3 Strong Two Openers
West deals

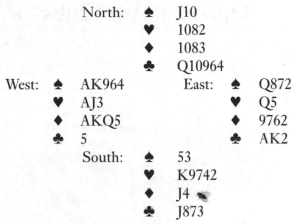

	North:	♠	J10			
		♥	1082			
		♦	1083			
		♣	Q10964			
West:	♠	AK964		East:	♠	Q872
	♥	AJ3			♥	Q5
	♦	AKQ5			♦	9762
	♣	5			♣	AK2
	South:	♠	53			
		♥	K9742			
		♦	J4			
		♣	J873			

West opens '2 Spades', having 21 points and only 4 losers.
North says 'No Bid'.
East having 11 points, 4 Spades and 8 losers, jumps to '4 No Trumps', asking how many Aces her opening partner holds.
South says 'No Bid'.
West replies '5 Spades' (3 Aces).
East happily bids '5 No Trumps'.
West replies '6 Hearts' (2 Kings).
They are missing 1 King, so East makes a final bid of '6 Spades', which is played by West.

12

Opening Two Clubs

The most exciting bid is when your partner opens by saying 2 Clubs. This means that she has at least 23 points in her hand. It does not mean that she wants to play in Clubs (she might not hold any) but it is merely a point count. Partner should *keep the bidding open for at least two rounds, preferably to game.* With very few points (under 3) she will give the negative response of 2 Diamonds, and then on her next bid (however bad it is, as her partner already knows that she has a poor hand) give her best suit or No Trumps. However, if the opener only had 23/24 points and a balanced hand, and the response was 2

Diamonds, he may bid 2 No Trumps to say that that is as far as they can go, and the responder can then say, 'No Bid' and not continue to game.

Hopefully, you will once again be able to use the Blackwood Convention (4 No Trumps) and go on to make a Slam.

The point about trying to make a Slam is that you get a tremendous amount of points above the line, as well as counting the points for your contracted number of tricks under the line.

For calling and making a Small Slam, non-vulnerable	500 points
For calling and making a Small Slam vulnerable	750 points
For calling and making a Grand Slam, non-vulnerable	1000 points
For calling and making a Grand Slam vulnerable	1500 points

So, if you bid and made a Grand Slam in 7 Spades and were vulnerable, you would score 1500 above the line and 210 below the line!

Example 1   Opening Two Clubs

North deals

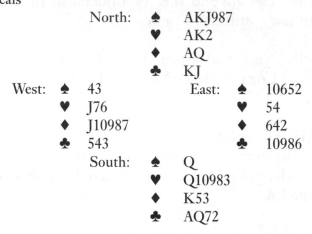

North: ♠ AKJ987
          ♥ AK2
          ♦ AQ
          ♣ KJ

West: ♠ 43   East: ♠ 10652
       ♥ J76   ♥ 54
       ♦ J10987   ♦ 642
       ♣ 543   ♣ 10986

South: ♠ Q
          ♥ Q10983
          ♦ K53
          ♣ AQ72

Even though his best suit is Spades, North opens '2 Clubs', (25 points and 4 Losing Tricks).

East and West will not attempt to bid.

South, with 13 points, responds with his longest suit saying '2 Hearts'. (This a positive bid.)

North now bids his good suit, '2 Spades'.

However, South doesn't like Spades and mentions his 4 card suit, bidding '3 Clubs'.

North re-bids his Spades (as he has 6 of them he could bid them 3 times), '3 Spades'.

South re-bids his Hearts, to show that he has 5 of them, '4 Hearts'.

North, as he has 3 Hearts, which make up the required 8 for trumps, goes to '4 No Trumps', agreeing with the last suit that has been bid by his partner ('let's try for a Slam in Hearts').

South responds '5 Diamonds' (1 Ace).

North ploughs on, bidding '5 No Trumps'.

South replies '6 Diamonds' (1 King).

North now knows that all 4 Aces and all 4 Kings are in their joint hands – so he, triumphantly, jumps to a Grand Slam, bidding '7 Hearts', which will be played by South. This is unfortunate, because the best suit will be exposed on the table, making it easier for their opponents – but I don't think, in this case, there will be any problem.

Example 2　　Opening 2 Clubs

East deals

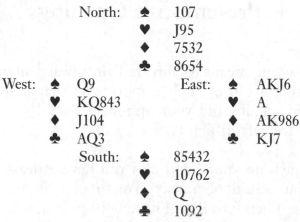

North:　♠　107
　　　　♥　J95
　　　　♦　7532
　　　　♣　8654

West:　♠　Q9　　　　East:　♠　AKJ6
　　　♥　KQ843　　　　　　♥　A
　　　♦　J104　　　　　　　♦　AK986
　　　♣　AQ3　　　　　　　♣　KJ7

South:　♠　85432
　　　　♥　10762
　　　　♦　Q
　　　　♣　1092

East starts by bidding '2 Clubs' (she has 23 points and only 4 Losers).

North and South do not bid.

West, with 14 points and 7 Losers, responds '2 Hearts'.

East now bids 3 Diamonds because she has 5 of them.

West repeats her Hearts, as she has no other 4 card suit to mention and to show that she has 5 of them, '3 Hearts'.

East is not at all keen on Hearts and re-bids her Diamonds, '4 Diamonds'.

West bows to her partner, knowing that East must have 5 Diamonds, as she has bid them twice, and she does, after all, have 3 Diamonds and 2 of them are Honours, and says '4 No Trumps', meaning 'I agree Diamonds and how many Aces have you in your hand?'

East responds '5 Spades' (3 Aces).

West, knowing that they have all 4 Aces, can either bid '6 Diamonds' (a Small Slam) or '5 No Trumps' asking for Kings, in which case if East has only 2 Kings and replies '6 Hearts' she would have to bid '7 Diamonds' with a King lurking in one of the enemies' hands. However, luck is with her and the reply of '6 Spades' means that she can happily go to '7 Diamonds'.

13

Pre-emptive Openings

To 'pre-empt' means to 'forestall' or 'thwart' an opponent, by making a bid at such a high level that it makes any ordinary opening bid your opponent would have liked to make extremely difficult.

If you pick up your hand and you have at least 7 of one suit, you would obviously like to play in that suit as Trumps. Therefore if you have 6-10 points, you open the bidding with <u>3</u> of the long suit. This is 'Length but not Strength'.

The opponents should only bid over you if they have really good opening hands and a 5 or 6 card suit.

The partner of the pre-emptive opener can put her up in the bid suit if she has at least 2 of that suit (preferably 3) and 10+ points. She can only change to another suit if she has at least 16 points and her new suit is a 5 or 6 card one, because, remember, the opener is weak and has specified the suit she wishes to be trumps.

If an opponent has made the first bid before you, and you have 7 of a suit and 6-10 points, the only way you can show your partner what you hold in your hand, is by jumping 3. For example, Opponent bids 1 Spade; you, with 7 Clubs and 8 points, bid 4 Clubs.

If either partnership has made an ordinary opening bid, the second player in that partnership, who has 7 of a suit in her hand, will not pre-empt her partner.

For example, Opener, having 13 points, says 1 Heart; her partner has 7 Diamonds and 9 points but she will *not* bid 4 Diamonds, merely 2 Diamonds, although she may jump later in the bidding to show her length. Obviously one doesn't want to force up one's partner, only the opponents.

Surprisingly, the pre-emptive opener will find she has very few losing tricks, in spite of her few points, because of the distribution.

If you have opened with this Weak call and no-one overcalls – you have a fairly nasty situation, but at least you have 7 trumps in your hand and have stopped the opponents from bidding.

The point of this pre-empt is to 'freeze out' your opponents, so that in order to bid higher than you, they may over-reach themselves and fail in their contract. However, they may have many more points than you and your partner and you are prepared to go down to stop them gaining a significant score. The rule of 500 says – 'you can lose 2 tricks, vulnerable, doubled, which equals 500 points; or, 3 tricks, non-vulnerable, doubled, which also equals 500 points. (I know you have not yet learned doubling scoring, but just accept this at the moment, please.)

Example 1   Pre-empt

South deals

		North:	♠	Q4			
			♥	AQ			
			♦	QJ10987			
			♣	K32			
West:	♠	KJ75			East:	♠	A932
	♥	63				♥	105
	♦	52				♦	K643
	♣	AQ964				♣	875
		South:	♠	1086			
			♥	KJ98742			
			♦	A			
			♣	J10			

South has 7 Hearts in his hand but only 9 points; however, he does have only 7 Losers, so he opens the bidding with '3 Hearts'.

West needs to have really good points to enter the bidding and, therefore, has to pass.

North, with 14 points, only 7 Losing Tricks and 2 good Hearts, puts up his partner to '4 Hearts'.

East with only 7 points has to say 'No Bid'.

The auction stops there.

Example 2   Pre-empt
West deals

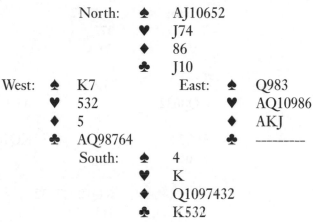

North: ♠ AJ10652
        ♥ J74
        ♦ 86
        ♣ J10

West: ♠ K7   East: ♠ Q983
       ♥ 532   ♥ AQ10986
       ♦ 5   ♦ AKJ
       ♣ AQ98764   ♣ ----------

South: ♠ 4
        ♥ K
        ♦ Q1097432
        ♣ K532

West opens '3 Clubs' as she has 9 points and only 6 Losing Tricks.
North, with only 7 points, passes.
East has 16 points and, therefore, enough to change the suit – particularly as she hates Clubs – so she says '3 Hearts'.
South also has a pre-emptive hand, but realises that it would be foolish to enter the bidding at this stage, because if he bids 4 Diamonds, it is more likely that he will push up West or East to bid a game.
However, West, knowing that her partner is strong and with 3 small Hearts, bids a game anyway, even though he has 9 instead of the 10 points, '4 Hearts'.
As East is so strong she might think of bidding 4 No Trumps and trying for a slam in Hearts, but, as she knows that West is weak, she will probably leave it in the 4 Hearts.

Note that it is odd how often, if one player has a long suit, the others also have funny distribution.

Example 3 — Overcalling with a pre-empt
East deals

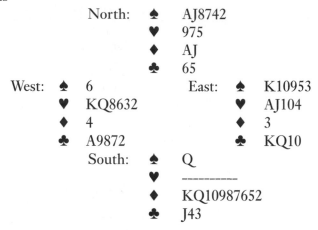

		North:	♠	AJ8742			
			♥	975			
			♦	AJ			
			♣	65			

West: ♠ 6   East: ♠ K10953
     ♥ KQ8632   ♥ AJ104
     ♦ 4   ♦ 3
     ♣ A9872   ♣ KQ10

         South: ♠ Q
               ♥ ----------
               ♦ KQ10987652
               ♣ J43

East opens '1 Spade', as she has 13 points and only 6 losers.

South has 9 Diamonds, 8 points and 5 losers, so overcalls and jumps to '4 Diamonds' (having to go up 3 to show length).

West, with only 5 losers and 9 points, replies to her opening partner by bidding '4 Hearts'.

North, with 10 points and good support in his partner's Diamonds, bids a game, '5 Diamonds'.

East likes partner's suit, but feels she can't bid 5 Hearts.

South passes.

West, conscious of her good losers, and also that her partner opened, throws her hat over the windmill and bids '5 Hearts'.

Either North or South could bid '6 Diamonds', even though they have only 18 points between them. But if they are wise, they will both say 'No Bid', because they must lose 2 Clubs, unless they can discard them on another suit. However, they may well continue in order to foil East and West.

14

Strong Pre-emptive Openings and the Jump Shift, Changing Suits and Jumping in Partner's Suit

You have now learned what you should do if you have at least seven cards in one suit and 6-10 points.

If you pick up your hand and you have these seven cards, but have 11+ points, it is no longer a Weak hand, so you must bid one of that suit and, if you get the opportunity, at your next bid – jump. Your partner will then know that you are *very* keen to play in that suit.

Now, supposing your opponent has already opened the bidding with 1 of a suit (or No Trumps) and you were sitting there panting to bid your seven card suit. The answer is, if you have 11+ points, merely bid normally: i.e. opponent: 1H; you, with 7 Diamonds and 12 points, 2 Diamonds.

Doing A Jump Shift If your opponent or your partner opens and you have at least 16 points you can show what you hold in your hand by jumping and shifting into another suit. For example: Opponent opens 1 Heart, you have 16 points and 5 Spades, so you bid 2 Spades – a Jump, because 1 Spade would be the normal bid over the 1 Heart.

Jumping In Partner's Suit Supposing your partner opens 1 Diamond and you have at least 4 of her Diamonds and 10 or more points, you should reply with 3 Diamonds.

Going From One Level To Another Your partner opens 1 Spade. You do not like Spades, but have 5 nice Diamonds. Since you will have to bid at the next level, saying 2 Diamonds, you need at least 9 points to bid that 2 Diamonds. If you only had 6-8 points, you could only keep the bidding open by saying 1 No Trump, hopefully with no singletons and evenish distribution.

Replying With No Trumps If your partner has opened the bidding with either a suit or a No Trump and you have 10-12 points and evenish distribution, reply 2 No Trumps or with 13-18 points, reply 3 No Trumps.

Changing Suit If your partner opens the bidding and you neither reply with a No Trump nor with her bid suit, but mention another suit, this is Forcing (1 Diamond to 1 Heart, or 1 Spade to 2 Clubs). *Any change of suit is Forcing.* Equally, if your partner does not repeat her opening suit nor support you in your suit, but bids a completely different one, then you are forced to reply.

Example 1   Strong pre-empt
North deals

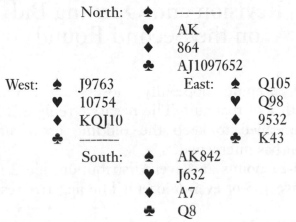

North: ♠ --------
        ♥ AK
        ♦ 864
        ♣ AJ1097652

West: ♠ J9763   East: ♠ Q105
       ♥ 10754   ♥ Q98
       ♦ KQJ10   ♦ 9532
       ♣ --------   ♣ K43

South: ♠ AK842
        ♥ J632
        ♦ A7
        ♣ Q8

North opens '1 Club' with 8 Clubs and more than 10 points.
East says 'No Bid'.
South responds '1 Spade', (remember, a change of suit is forcing).
West says 'No Bid'.
North now makes a jump bid to show that he has a long suit and really wants that suit to be trumps, saying, '3 Clubs'.
South should probably now bid '3 No Trumps', as the long suit in Clubs will be very useful in a No Trump game. (If you have to make a choice between bidding 5 in a minor suit in order to make a game, or only bidding 3 in No Trumps, it is often better to choose the latter.)

QUESTION

What would you bid for the above example?

15

Revision and Opening Bid on the Second Round

With 19-22 points, hopefully 4 losers, and a 5 card suit, open with 2 of that suit. The negative reply is 2 NT and must be called to keep the bidding open, unless an opponent has intervened.

With 20-22 points and even distribution, bid 2 NT. You could have 4, 5 or even 6 losers. The negative response is No Bid.

With at least 23 points and 4 or fewer losers, bid 2 Clubs (even if you have no Clubs). The negative response is 2 Diamonds and bidding should continue for at least two rounds and preferably to game.

If you think that you might be able to call and get a Slam: a Small Slam is 12 tricks - bid 6; a Grand Slam is all 13 tricks - bid 7; you need to have good HCP between you, 32-33 for a Small Slam, 34-37 for a Grand Slam.

A Grand Slam. Hassall

But, remember, that having few Losers is even more important than the HCP. To find out whether you hold all 4 Aces between you, use the Blackwood Convention and bid 4 NT; replies are 5C = 0 or 4 aces, 5D = 1 Ace, 5 Hearts = 2 Aces, 5 Spades = 3 Aces.

If you wish to explore further and find out about the Kings – bid 5 NT; replies are 6C = 0 or 4 Kings, 6D = 1 King, 6H = 2 Kings, 6 Spades = 3 Kings.

With 7 of one suit and 6-10 points, open the bidding with 3 of that suit (or, if you are brave, overcall the opposition's opening bid by going up 3, e.g. 1 Spade to 4 Diamonds). To reply, your partner needs a good opening hand, 10 points and at least 2 of the bid suit to raise in that suit and 16+ points to change the suit. The opposition need a good opening hand and a 5 or 6 card suit to enter the bidding. If you have 7 of one suit and 11+ points, open 1 of that suit and then jump next time.

Your Second Bid Supposing that you either do not have those necessary 12 points to open the bidding for your side, or you have more than 7 Losing Tricks and your hand is not suitable for a No Trump bid. You have said "No Bid" and your partner has not opened. When the bidding comes back to you, you could now open with your best suit. This will alert your partner to the fact that you are not quite as good as you would like, but have either 8 Losers and 12 or more points, or 7 Losers and less than 12 points.

QUIZ

1. Your partner has opened 1 Spade and you have 11 points, no 5 card suits, and no singleton, nor void.
   What do you respond?

2. You have called 4 Hearts but only made 7 tricks – you and your partner are vulnerable. How many points do the opposition score?

3. Your partner has bid Clubs, but your opponents have won the bidding and Trumps are Spades. You have 1 Club in your own hand, the 10; it is your first lead.
   What do you put down?

4. You have bid 1 Heart and your partner has replied 1 No Trump (with no intervening bid from the opposition).
   How many points and what distribution do you think she has?

5. You have 8 Losing Tricks, 12 HCP, no singletons, and fairly even distribution. Can you make a bid:
   (a) If you are the first bidder on the table? And with what?
   (b) If your opponents have opened the bidding, what should you say?

6. Your partner has opened 1 No Trump; you have only 4 points and 5 Clubs.
   (a) What do you respond?
   (b) Would your partner make another bid?

7. Your opponents opened 1 Heart, her partner replied 1 Spade (you and your partner have said No Bid), and the opener has now made a re-bid of 1 NT.
   How many points does she hold?

8. You are thrilled!; your partner has opened 2 Clubs; unfortunately, you have only 2 points and 5 Spades.
   (a) What do you bid the first time?
   (b) The second?

9. Your partner has bid 1 Diamond; you have 17 points in your hand and 5 Clubs.
   How do you respond?

10. You pick up your hand and you have 8 Clubs and 12 points.
    What do you bid?

16

What Should You Lead?

You may well have been puzzled as to which card and suit you should put down on the table when it is your lead.

Try to lead a suit if your partner has bid it. She is probably strong in it. And don't lead a suit that the opponents have bid.

Although this is obviously very important if you are the first person to play, you can also follow these rules throughout the game if possible. Always remember to return a suit that has been led by your partner – what he has led *means* something!

Returning your Partner's Lead.

FOR SUIT CONTRACTS, lead:

1. A SINGLETON although, obviously, not in the Trump suit, unless you hold only a useless trump and know it will never take a trick.

2. A DOUBLETON (only 2 cards of the same suit) lead the Higher card, then next time the lower one. If you held a Jack and a 6, you would lead the Jack, then the 6. Exceptions are: if the Higher Doubleton were a King or a Queen, play a different suit, because it might be better to save them in case they might take a trick late, and some people when holding only 2 cards in a suit, namely the Ace and the King, lead the King first and then the Ace.

3. ACES With an Ace in a suit, you must lead the Ace unless it is a doubleton Ace/King. If you want to save that Ace lead another suit.

4. 3 CARD SUITS

a) Lead the top of the touching Honour cards.

b) With only one Honour card, lead the bottom card, although if the Honour is an Ace you must lead it.

c) If you don't have an Honour card in the suit you wish to lead, because maybe your partner has bid it, play Middle – Up – Down (MUD) to show the difference between this and a Doubleton.

5. With 4 Card Or Longer Suits Again, as with 3 Card suits, you should lead the top of the touching Honours from sequence combinations, fourth from the top otherwise,e.g. K, 6, 4, **3**, 2; 10, 8, 5, **3**; **K**, Q, J, 6; **J**, 10, 4.

If you have 3 Honour cards, with two touching, lead the higher of the two touching, e.g. K, **J** 10; **K**, Q, 10. With useless cards you will have to play MUD: the 2nd highest followed by the highest and finally the lowest, e.g. 8, 6, 5, 4, 2 (you would lead the 6, then 8 and then 2).

6. In No Trumps Lead 4th highest *unless* you have three Honours in a long suit, e.g. A K J x x, or K Q 10 x x – in which case lead your highest Honour in order to set up this long suit, before your opponents have chosen to play all the other suits and leave out your nice winners.

Precis

For Suit Contracts, lead:
> Your partner's suit, or
> A Singleton, or
> With an Ace, lead it, or
> Bottom to an Honour, or
> Top of touching Honour, or sequence*, or
> A Doubleton – High/Low, or
> Middle of rubbish.

For No Trump Contracts, lead:
Fourth highest of longest suit, unless, you have three honours in a 4+ card suit i.e. **A**, K, J, 6, 5 or **K**, Q, 10, 9, 6.

*N.B. When responding to a suit with a sequence, you do the opposite, and play the lowest card to tell partner you have at least one other card in that suit, above the one you have played.

77

QUIZ

Now let's see if you understand why the lead can give further information.

In the following three different examples, imagine that you are playing in a suit contract, sitting East, and have won the bidding. From South's lead, you should be able to assess what he holds in the suit that is led and, therefore, act appropriately yourself. All the cards are in the same suit, but it is not the trump suit. It would be a good idea to lay out each set of cards, you playing as East.

Example 1   South leads the 10,
                   West (as Dummy) lays down 8, 5, 3, 2,
                   North ??
                   East (yourself) K, Q, 9.

Example 2   South leads the 5,
                   West (Dummy) lays down K, J, 4, 3,
                   North ??
                   East (yourself) A, Q, 10, 2.

Example 3   South leads the King,
                   West (Dummy) lays down J, 7, 6,
                   North ??
                   East (yourself) A, 9, 3.

Which card should you lead in a suit contract?

(1) 6 2	(2) 7 3	(3) 8 5 2	(4) 9 6 5 4
(5) 8 5 4 3 2	(6) 10 9 3 2	(7) 10 6 3 2	(8) J 10
(9) J 9 8	(10) Q J 7 2	(11) J 9 7 6	(12) Q 10 5 4
(13) Q 10 9	(14) K Q J 5	(15) K J 10 6 4	(16) A J 6 5 4

17

Revision and Revoking

You should open 1NT if you have 12-14 points and even distribution. The even distribution is important – so a void, a singleton or an unsatisfactory doubleton could cause problems as this bid does not force a response and, anyway, partner could have shortages in your poor suit(s).

To bid a suit you must have at least 4 cards in that suit – with 5 of that suit repeat it, with 6 bid it for the third time. But remember: with two 4 card suits, bid the lower ranking first; with one 5 card suit and one 4 card suit, bid the 5 card first; and if your partner does not support you in that suit, try the 4 card suit, they might prefer it. You can then repeat the first suit, if you can, to tell them it is a 5 card suit.

With two 5 card suits, bid the higher ranking first, then the lower; then if you get the chance, repeat the second suit, e.g. with 5 Spades and 5 Diamonds, first bid is a Spade, second bid is a Diamond, the third bid is another Diamond; thus your partner will know that both suits are 5 card ones.

With 15-19 points and a balanced hand, open with a four card suit, and bid No Trumps on your second bid. If you have 15/16 points bid 1 No Trump, if possible; with 17/18 bid 2 No Trumps; and with 19 points bid 3 No Trumps.

Responses with a balanced hand to your partner's opening bid of either a suit or a No Trump: with 6-9 points, bid 1 No Trump; with 10-12, bid 2NT; with 13-18, bid 3NT; with 19 or more, explore Slam.

Responses to the 1 No Trump opener from your partner: with 5 cards (or more) in a suit, do the weakness take-out: 0-10 points, bidding the suit at the 2 level (opener must pass); 11+ points, bid 3 of the 5 card suit (game must be considered).

Be careful not to be so enthusiastic if your partner opens, for example, 1 Heart. If you have a fistful of them, and make a bid of 4 Hearts, this is a game call and means that your partner will probably stop at that game call and not try for a Slam. It would be better to bid 3 Hearts and hope that your partner will at least go on to 4 Hearts or, more hopefully, to 4 No Trumps.

REVOKING – this is when you are unfortunate enough to make a mistake and do not follow suit, even though you are holding at least one of that suit in your hand. There are various penalties awarded for this offence, but, generally, in social bridge the other players will realise that it was a genuine error and allow you to play the correct card. If a fine is imposed it could be as much as two tricks to the other side, but let's hope you have generous opponents.

a Revoke.   Hassall

80

QUIZ

1. You have called a Small Slam but have only made 8 tricks. How many points will your opponents score if you are:
   (a) non-vulnerable?
   (b) vulnerable?

2. Your partner has opened 1 Diamond; you have replied 1 Spade and she has then re-bid 2 No Trumps. How many HCP do you think she holds?

3. The opponent just before you has opened 1 Heart; you have 7 Diamonds and 8 HCP. What do you bid?

4. Your partner has opened the bidding with 1 Club; you have 14 points, no singletons and no five card suit. What do you respond?

5. You have 21 points and no five card suit and no singletons.
   (a) What do you bid?
   (b) Your partner has only 2 points and no 5 card suit. What is her response?

6. You open 1 No Trump; your partner replies 3 Diamonds (with no intervening bid). How many points do you presume she has?

7. Your partner has bid Hearts, but the opposition have won the bidding and Clubs are now trumps; you hold the Ace and 5 of Hearts; it is you to lead first. What do you put down?

8. Your partner has opened 2 Clubs, so she must have at least 23 points and 4 or less Losers (exciting!); you have 10 points, 8 Losing Tricks, and your best suit is Hearts (you have 6 of them).
   (a) What do you bid? and,
   (b) if your partner re-bids 3 Hearts, what do you then say?

Example   Revision of Slam bidding
South deals

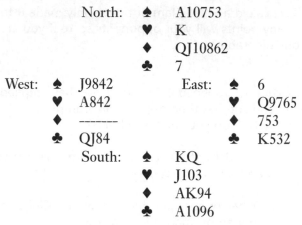

North: ♠   A10753
         ♥   K
         ♦   QJ10862
         ♣   7

West: ♠   J9842   East: ♠   6
       ♥   A842   ♥   Q9765
       ♦   -------   ♦   753
       ♣   QJ84   ♣   K532

South: ♠   KQ
        ♥   J103
        ♦   AK94
        ♣   A1096

South opens '1 Club', having 17 points and 7 losers, but no 5 card suit. Clubs are the lower of his 4 card suits and he has too many points to open a No Trump and show his shape.

West says 'No Bid'.

North bids '1 Diamond'.

East says 'No Bid'.

South jumps to '2 No Trumps' to show his 17 points and even distribution.

North repeats his Diamonds, bidding '3 Diamonds'.

South, with 4 of his partner's Diamonds, bids '4 No Trumps', asking for Aces, and agreeing Diamonds.

North replies '5 Diamonds'.

South, realising they are missing 1 Ace, can either say 'No Bid', or be brave and go up to '6 Diamonds' and a Small Slam.

18

Penalty Double

This is really saying "I know you can't get this contract, because I have points and some of your suit and have worked out that you have gone too high for your bid"!

It is a penalty double if it is at a fairly high level and if your partner has already made a bid, you can only double a *suit* bid by your opponent; to double a pre-emptive bid you must have a really good opening hand, preferably 16 points.

To double a No Trump you must have at least 16 points, which is explained at the end of this chapter.

Therefore, if your opponent opens 1 Heart and you have been waiting to bid the same thing, having 13 points and 5 Hearts – resist the impulse to say anything – merely grin quietly to yourself and bide your time!

OPPOSITION	YOU	OPPOSITION	PARTNER
1 Heart	No Bid	2 Hearts	2 Spades
3 Hearts	No Bid	4 Hearts	No Bid
No Bid	Double!!!		

You realise your partner has an opening bid, or at least an overcall, and as you yourself have 13 points and all those Hearts, the poor opposition are highly unlikely to make their contract!

A Penalty Double can sometimes be the only way to show displeasure. For instance, if both partnerships appear to have equally good hands and have been busily bidding up to game, but one side has a higher value suit than the other, and will obviously be able to reach a game bid before their opponents.

If 4 Spades were bid over the opponents, who might be left grinding their teeth in 4 Hearts, the opponents only defence is to Double and hope that, because they have good hands themselves, the nasty couple, who won the Contract, will lose.

You should be careful not to double them, carelessly, into game.

For example, their bidding has stopped at 3 Diamonds and you have good Diamonds and say "Double". If they are successful and get their contract you will have doubled them into the equivalent of 6 Diamonds (a Game, but not a Slam) and they will score 120 below the line, and 50 above the line for the 'insult' suffered by them as you doubted their efficiency!

Also, be aware that, if they have bid another suit, and you and your partner are not adequately covered in this second suit, they may simply change to the second suit – and you will have lost any element of surprise! Sometimes it is better to stay quiet and just get them down!

Your partner does NOT have to reply to a penalty double.

Penalty doubles are great fun for you (the doubler) but not for your opponents! The important thing to remember is that you must resist the impulse to double too early. Try and wait until the opposition have happily agreed a suit and reached game – then you can double them without the risk of doubling them into a game.

The point about doubling is that a great number of points can be gained by the doubling team:

Non-vulnerable:	100 for the first trick down,
	200 for the 2nd and 3rd,
	300 for any subsequent one
Vulnerable	200 for the first trick down and
	300 for each subsequent one

Whereas, if the partnership who have been doubled get their contract they get their scores doubled plus that 50 (for the insult), e.g. 4 Hearts doubled = 240 + 50, which is not a tremendous amount. Any overtricks won by the doubled partnership score above the line, 100 per trick if non-vulnerable, and 200 per trick if vulnerable.

Redoubling – which can be done by the partnership bidding the contract, after they have been doubled – means that they consider that they *will* make their contract. This quadruples the points both for losing and gaining their contract and the 'insult' becomes 100 points.

SCORING QUIZ

Write the answers to the quiz on the next page on a scorecard, showing scores for N/S and E/W, and what were the scores and final result of the rubber. Treat it as a real game, so everyone starts off non-vulnerable:

1. North   bids 2 Spades,   doubled   makes 7 tricks
2. West   bids 3 Hearts,   doubled   makes 10 tricks
3. East   bids 4 Spades,   doubled   makes 6 tricks
4. South   bids 2 Clubs,   doubled   makes 11 tricks
5. North   bids 3 Hearts,   doubled   makes 5 tricks
6. West   bids 6 Clubs,   doubled   makes 13 tricks

Example 1   Penalty Double
North deals

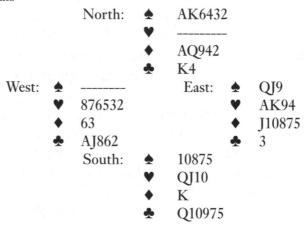

North:	♠	AK6432
	♥	—————
	♦	AQ942
	♣	K4

West: ♠ —————   East: ♠ QJ9
      ♥ 876532   ♥ AK94
      ♦ 63   ♦ J10875
      ♣ AJ862   ♣ 3

South:	♠	10875
	♥	QJ10
	♦	K
	♣	Q10975

North opens '1 Spade'.

East, having only 7 losers and a 5 card suit, overcalls '2 Diamonds'.

South supports his partner and bids '2 Spades'.

West does not have enough points to change suit, and doesn't like Diamonds, so says 'No Bid'.

North, with only 3 losers, goes mad and jumps to game in Spades, '4 Spades', although he should have said 'No Bid', as his partner bid 'I up/shut up'.

East then 'Doubles'.

South could now evade the Double by calling '5 Clubs', but if he did, West could 'Double' him.

North cannot bid his second suit, as East has already bid Diamonds – dilemma! Who will win???

Example 2   Penalty Double

East deals

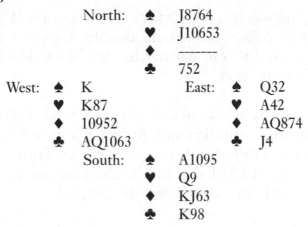

North: ♠   J8764
    ♥   J10653
    ♦   -------
    ♣   752

West: ♠   K   East: ♠   Q32
    ♥   K87   ♥   A42
    ♦   10952   ♦   AQ874
    ♣   AQ1063   ♣   J4

South: ♠   A1095
    ♥   Q9
    ♦   KJ63
    ♣   K98

East bids '1 Diamond', having 13 points and 7 losers.

South, also with 13 points, cannot overcall as he does not hold a 5 card suit, and now to bid a No Trump he would need 16 points. He therefore passes.

West, with 12 points, 7 losers, and 4 of her partner's Diamonds, jumps to '3 Diamonds'.

North says 'No Bid'.

East goes to a game in Diamonds, '5 Diamonds'.

South, who has been lying low with her 4 Diamonds, now erupts and says 'Double'.

The bidding will now go round again in case West, North or East wish to bid.

It is difficult for E/W, at this very high level, to think of changing into another suit, but this bid of 5 Diamonds, now doubled, is doubtful.

Doubling a No Trump

If your opponent opens with a No Trump and you have at least 16 points you should double. THIS IS A PENALTY DOUBLE, even if your partner has not bid and you are still at the bottom level.

You do not have to hold a No Trump hand, although you could overbid with this, but, in fact, a long suit with good high cards is infinitely better; if the 1 No Trump doubled stays as the last bid you will be the first one to lead and might be able to make all of your long suit.

The partner of the opposition opener will try very hard to get out of this contract but there are times when this is impossible (for example, if she has very few points and no 5 card suit).

The partner of the doubler will say nothing unless she has very few points herself and at least a 5 card suit and fears that the opposition will successfully make their 1 No Trump doubled (now worth 80 points under the line and 50 points for the insult), in which case she would do a weakness take-out. If, however, the doubler's partner has at least 6 points she will not bid because she knows that the doubler has at least 16 and that, therefore, at the very minimum, they have 22 points between them, and the opposition have only 18 at the most and are unlikely to make their contract.

Ignore this – unless you are playing with someone who is very 'on the ball' and knows the Laws of the English Bridge Union backwards: if the bidding has gone 1 No Trump, No Bid, No Bid, Double – this double is for take-out, not penalty and your partner must give her best suit.

However, I don't think that EBU Laws are very seriously practised by social players.

Example 1   Penalty Double of a No Trump

North deals

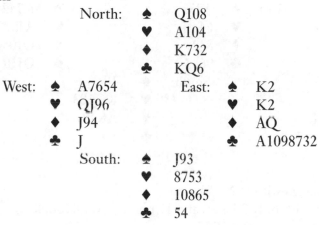

North: ♠ Q108
        ♥ A104
        ♦ K732
        ♣ KQ6

West: ♠ A7654   East: ♠ K2
       ♥ QJ96   ♥ K2
       ♦ J94   ♦ AQ
       ♣ J   ♣ A1098732

South: ♠ J93
        ♥ 8753
        ♦ 10865
        ♣ 54

North with 14 points and even distribution, opens '1 No Trump'.
East has 16 points and a long suit of Clubs; rather than overcalling with 2 Clubs, she says 'Double'.
South has only 1 point and no 5 card suit and is unable to extract his partner from the 'double'.
West, although she has a 5 card suit, says 'No Bid' because she knows that she and her partner must have at least 25 points between them and that, therefore, poor North can only rustle up 15 points between himself and his dummy and is, therefore, singularly unlikely to make his contract.
North, unable to bid anything else, has to grit his teeth and hope to go down as little as possible.

Example 2   Penalty Double of a No Trump

East deals

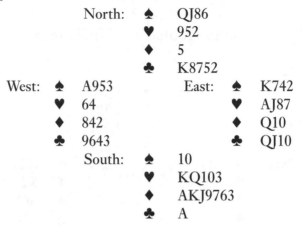

North: ♠ QJ86
         ♥ 952
         ♦ 5
         ♣ K8752

West: ♠ A953   East: ♠ K742
       ♥ 64   ♥ AJ87
       ♦ 842   ♦ Q10
       ♣ 9643   ♣ QJ10

South: ♠ 10
        ♥ KQ103
        ♦ AKJ9763
        ♣ A

East opens with '1 No Trump'.

South with only 3 losers and 17 points, says 'Double'.

West sadly says 'No Bid'.

North has only 6 points and could bid 2 Clubs. However, he should say 'No Bid' and leave the unfortunate East/West pair to their doom. It might be a good idea to bid the above cards, firstly, continuing on as if North did indeed say '2 Clubs', and discover in which contract you finish and how it would be played.

Secondly, play out the cards with East having bid '1 No Trump', doubled, and see in which contract North/South make the greater score.

19

Take-Out Doubles

I have thought long and hard about whether I should include this particular aspect of play. I am sorry because it is definitely a 'contraption', but I think that it is so very useful that you really need to know about Take-Out Doubles. They are a way of finding out what your partner has in their hand and, also, giving him/her information.

You can do a take-out double with an opening hand after your opponent has made a bid in a suit (<u>not</u> a No Trump bid) and YOUR PARTNER HAS NOT MADE A BID.

Ideally, you should be very short in the opponent's bid suit, but be all right in the other three suits – so what you are saying to your partner is "tell me your best suit and I can support you in any of them – except the one which has been bid by the opposition".

It is made at the one, two or three level, this last with a really good point count, preferably 16, after a pre-emptive bid by your opponent.

Your partner MUST reply irrespective of her number of points, unless:

a) there has been an intervening bid or a redouble from the partner of the first opposition bidder – although this is generally frowned upon, as the doubler really wanted to know what was in her partner's hand or,

b) she has a very strong holding in the enemy's suit and your double would then, happily, become the equivalent of a penalty double!

The partner of the take-out doubler will respond at the cheapest level with 0-8 HCP bidding her best suit (which might even be a 3 card suit, if no 4 card suit is held outside the enemy suit); with 9-12 HCP she will jump, to show that she is quite strong; with 13+, she will go to game level. Or, she could bid 1NT with even distribution, 6-9 HCP and a stopper in the enemy's bid suit; 2NT with (as usual) 10/12 HCP and the stopper, and 3NT with 13/18 HCP and good stoppers.

QUIZ on all Doubling:

1. Your opponent has opened 1 Diamond and you have 16 points and 5 Diamonds.
   (a) What should you bid? and
   (b) if they reach game in Diamonds, what do you do then?
2. You have 16 HCP: 4 Spades, 3 Clubs, 2 Diamonds (miserable ones), and 4 Hearts; your opponents open the bidding with 1 Diamond.
   (a) What do you bid?
   (b) if your partner then bids 2 Hearts, what do you then bid?
3. You have 14 points and your partner has replied 1NT to you; your opponents have reached 4 Hearts.
   Should you double?
4. You have doubled the opponents 6 Clubs and they are vulnerable and have only made 10 tricks.
   What do you score?
5. The opponents have opened 1 Spade and your partner has doubled.
   (a) What do you think she has in her hand?
   (b) If you have the King, Jack and two other Spades and 9 points, what should you respond to your partner?

6. You bid 3 Clubs and your opponent doubled you; you made your contract.
   What do you score?
7. Your partner has doubled the opponent's bid of 1 No Trump;
   You have 11 points and 5 Spades.
   What do you bid?

Example 1   Take-Out Doubles
South deals

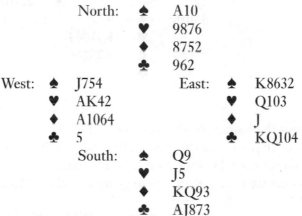

	North:	♠	A10
		♥	9876
		♦	8752
		♣	962

West: ♠ J754   East: ♠ K8632
♥ AK42   ♥ Q103
♦ A1064   ♦ J
♣ 5   ♣ KQ104

South: ♠ Q9
♥ J5
♦ KQ93
♣ AJ873

South bids '1 Club'.

West with 12 points, a shortage in Clubs, and adequate in the other 3 suits, does a 'take-out double', asking her partner to give her best suit.

North says 'No Bid'.

East with 11 points, jumps in her Spades, saying '2 Spades'.

South says 'No Bid'.

West, having 4 Spades, and knowing her partner has 9–12 points, bids '3 Spades'.

North says 'No Bid'.

East counts her losers and, realizing that they can get a game in Spades, bids '4 Spades'.

Example 2   Take-Out Doubles
West deals

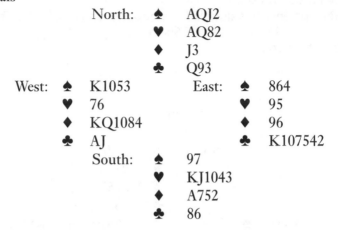

	North:	♠	AQJ2
		♥	AQ82
		♦	J3
		♣	Q93

West:	♠	K1053	East:	♠	864
	♥	76		♥	95
	♦	KQ1084		♦	96
	♣	AJ		♣	K107542

	South:	♠	97
		♥	KJ1043
		♦	A752
		♣	86

West opens the bidding with '1 Diamond'.

North with 16 points, could overcall by bidding 1 No Trump, but his Diamonds are poor. He therefore says 'Double'.

East does not have enough points to go up a level to '2 Clubs', so says 'No Bid'.

South, having 8 points, bids his best suit, '1 Heart'.

West having no response from her partner, says 'No Bid'.

North has only 6 losers, and having 4 of his partner's Hearts, jumps to '3 Hearts', because 2 Hearts would be '1 Up – Shut-Up'.

East again passes.

South calls '4 Hearts'.

20

Analysis

You have now learned the basic rules of Bridge. However, because you are so keen to get on with the bidding and the playing, you are not spending enough time working out what your hand can really do, and taking the other players' bidding into account. This is a very common fault and, I know, that there is nothing more irritating than someone who ponders over their hand for ages, while the rest of you start drumming your fingers on the table!

When you first pick up your dealt hand:

Count the High Card Points
Count your Losing Tricks

Look carefully at the score sheet and work out exactly what you and your opponents need to make a game and then always bid to your hand. In other words, if you have 60 below the line already, don't meekly stop at 1 No Trump, 2 Spades, 2 Hearts, 2 Diamonds or 2 Clubs, you might be able to get a Slam!

If you have a fantastic hand, or your partner does a jump bid, then always consider trying for a slam. To go down is infinitely better, in my opinion, than it is to boringly bid for your game and then make a slam – forfeiting all those lovely bonus points!

Remember what everyone has bid – not just your partner but the opponents as well – because if one of them has bid

Hearts, for example, you know that she has a good holding in that suit.

As soon as dummy has been put down (whether it is your partner or one of the opponents), you must pause and consider again. How are you going to make the tricks that are needed either to get your contract or to defeat the opponents' contract? The opposition, meanwhile, will be doing the same. As all of you can now see two hands and have (of course!) remembered the bidding, you should now have a fairly good idea of what is in whose hands.

Try and remember to check on the following:

WINNERS	between dummy and yourself
OPPORTUNITIES	to gain extra tricks
LOSING TRICK COUNT	for the 2 hands
DANGERS	those cards that are potentially lethal to you

Therefore, **W O L D**

W Inspect each suit and count how many tricks are absolutely foolproof, (unless you are extremely unlucky with an opponent's shortage if you are in a suit contract) e.g. if you have the A, K, Q that should be 3 certain tricks.

O If you are short in the number of tricks you need to make, work out how many extra you need and then look for your chances to make them. For example, you have bid 3 Spades, but can only see 7 obvious winners, so somehow you must make another 2. Remember you are not playing solo; you do have a partner and those 2 missing winning tricks just might be lurking in her hand.

In a No Trump contract, if you have a long suit, then you will probably make some, if not all, of the smaller cards in that suit; if you have split honours, e.g. A, K, J, 9, 5 in one hand and Q, 3, 2 in the other, you should be able to make five tricks. Just be careful to work out which hand you wish to end up in so that you can play the rest of the suit; for example, don't play the 3 to the A, and then the K to the 2 – because on your next lead of that suit you would have to play the Q and then be unable to get back into the other hand.

L You have used the Losing Trick Count to work out your own bidding and have estimated how many Losers your partner has by her bidding. Now, if she becomes the Dummy, you can see whether you were correct. Remember, even if you have more Losing Tricks together than you want, sometimes these are not infallible (is anything in Bridge?), so do not be disheartened.

D See which cards are absolutely necessary for you to win and which are not in your two hands. If the opponents have done any bidding there may be a clue as to where any of the missing cards are to be found. Note that if one of them has bid Hearts she must have at least 4 of them; if her next bid was Spades, you know that she has either 4 or 5 Hearts and 4 Spades; but, if she bid Spades followed by Hearts you know that her Spades are at least a 5 card suit. (Remember, with 4 card suits bid the lower first, with 5 card suits bid the higher.)

Also, remember not to play out all your top cards (particularly in a No Trump contract) and leave yourself stripped of potential winning cards. Sometimes it is necessary deliberately to allow the opponents to win, in order to set up later tricks for yourself.

21

Responding to Opening Bids, Finesses, Rules of 20, 14 and 11, and Discards

You should be aware that bids are:
Limit Bids or Forcing Bids

a) Limit Bids generally mean "do not continue to bid", going 1 up on the opener's bid suit (1 up = shut up). However, if the responder jumped in her opener's bid suit (e.g. 1 Club – 3 Clubs) or answered with a No Trump, the opener may continue to bid, as these are 'invitations'.

b) Forcing Bids: this is a change of suit even at the same level (1 Diamond – 1 Spade) and shows 6-15 points, while a new suit at the 2-level (1 Heart – 2 Clubs) shows 9-15 points. Do not do a jump-shift (1 Heart to 3 Clubs) unless you have 16+ points because it wastes bidding space and, as your partner must reply if you have changed suit, you can, if necessary, show a better hand than she might expect by jumping the next time.

Leading to Strength

After Dummy has been laid down, you and everyone else can see two hands. If you have the lead and are the player just before dummy, it is sometimes a good idea to lead up to a strong suit in dummy in case your partner would be able to overtake and win the trick. For example, Dummy has Spades K, J, 10, 9, 6. You do not have the Ace nor Queen of Spades, but your partner might, and she will be able to put one of them on the Dummy's card. So you lead a small Spade and wait to see what will happen. It is certainly worrying for your opponent unless he holds the winning cards in his hand – in which case he would win them anyway.

Finesses

Finesses are extremely important. Supposing you are the declarer and hold the A, Q, J, 10, 9 in one suit and, when dummy has been put down, you realise that the missing King must be hiding in one of the opponent's hands – how do you find out where it is? If you played out the Ace, whoever held the King would merely hold onto it and then be able to stop you playing out your Queen, Jack etc. What you must do is to take full advantage of the fact that you hold a card (the Ace) greater than the missing King. So you must 'lead up' to the Ace, but then not play it, unless the King falls. This gives you a 50% chance of winning

99

and, if not, the King will have been played and you can win the rest of that suit. If you finesse, you have a 50% chance of losing – if you meekly play the Ace you have a 100% chance of losing.

Finessing.   HASSALL

Example of a Finesse in Cards of One Suit

Dummy 8, 3, 2

West 7, 5   East K, 6, 4

Declarer A, Q, J, 10, 9

Declarer gets into Dummy with another suit and plays the 3, (remember, MUD: Middle – Up – Down).
If East plays her King, Declarer will take it with her Ace.
If East plays low, Declarer will take a chance and play her Queen.
When West plays the 7, Declarer knows that the King lies in East's hand, and knows her Ace will always sit over the King. When next in Dummy, she will play her 8, and eventually her 3 when East's King will have to fall, and Declarer takes it triumphantly with the Ace, and plays the other two cards of that suit.

Rule of 20
You should count your HCP plus the number of cards in your two longest suits. If the total comes to more than 20 open the bidding. You will find that the Losing Trick Count generally supports this.

Rule of 14
Only reply with a new suit to your partner's opening bid at the two-level when your points in the whole hand plus the number of cards in the new suit add up to 14 or more; if you have fewer points you can keep the bidding open by saying '1NT'.

Rule of 11
This is used when you are playing in a NT contract. When your partner leads the 4th highest of his suit, take away the value of his card (say the 6 of Diamonds) from 11 (in this case it equals 5). Once Dummy has been put down, you will be able to see how many Diamonds he has, higher than the 6. Supposing that Dummy has the 9 and the 10 of Diamonds, and you have the Ace and 7 in your hand, you realise that the declarer must have only one Diamond higher than that 6 in his hand.

If you are analytical and wonder why '11', the answer is that every suit in the pack consists of 13 cards. The Ace (or one) is promoted from its lowest position to become the highest ranking card in the suit. Therefore, the '2' becomes the lowest card – in other words the *face value* of each card is one more than its ranking within the suit (so, the Ace becomes not the 13th card, but the 14th). When a player leads fourth best he has three cards higher than the one he has led, take away three from fourteen and you arrive at eleven – clear as mud, or what?

Example

North Diamond 8 lead

West – declarer   East Diamond 10 9 6

South Diamond A 3

There are 3 higher Diamond cards than the 8 which was led, once dummy has been put down; you, at South, can see the 10 and the 9, and you have the Ace in your hand. Therefore, West, the declarer, cannot have any card higher than the 8 in her hand, so the answer is, if East plays either the 10, 9, or 6, you will overtake with the Ace and lead back the 3, to the missing King, Queen, and Jack, which must be in your partner's hand (4 diamond tricks won).

The Odds
If you have 8 cards in a particular suit between you and your partner, five are missing. How often will they break 3-2, or how often 4-1?

Turn the numbers back to front for the answer:
The 3/2 break happens $2/3$ of the time and the 4/1 break $1/4$ of the time.
With six cards missing, the 4/2 break occurs 2/4 (or $1/2$) the time; however the 3/3 break does not happen 3/3 (or 100% of the time), there is about a 1-in-3 chance.

8 Ever, 9 Never
With 8 trumps between you and your dummy, do a finesse if you are looking for a missing card (you have the A, K and are looking for the Q); with 9 trumps go for the drop, as there are only 4 out against you and there is a fair chance that your opponents have 2 each.

Discarding

Supposing you are unable to follow suit and you wish your partner at her next opportunity would lead a particular card in another suit, you attract her attention by throwing away a card in that longed-for suit, hoping that she will take the hint. There are various methods of doing this, either by throwing a low card, or making it even more obvious and jettisoning a high card.

QUIZ

What do you respond when your partner has made an opening bid?

1. After 1 No Trump opener with 5 Diamonds and 7 points?
2. After 1 Spade opener with 4 points and no 5 card suit?
3. After 1 No Trump with 6 Clubs and 12 points?
4. After 1 Heart opener with uneven distribution, 7 points and 3 Hearts?
5. After 1 Diamond opener with 10 points and 5 Clubs?
6. After 1 Club opener with 16 points and 5 Diamonds?
7. After 1 Spade opener with 14 points and 3 Spades and no singletons?
8. After 1 Heart opener with 5 Clubs, 2 Hearts, 3 Diamonds, 3 Spades and 8 points?
9. After 1 No Trump opener with 12 points and even distribution?
10. After 1 Spade opener with 3 points and 4 Spades?

22

Examples of
Bidding and Playing

Following are three examples of hands. Previously in this book I have merely given the bidding and suggested that you lay out the cards and play them out yourselves; now I have also written out how to play the cards in these examples. This is because now you have learned and understand so much about Bridge: Finessing, Leads, Blackwood, Weakness Take-Outs, Doubling, Overcalling with a No Trump and so much more. Of course, a tremendous amount depends on which card is led throughout every game and the Defenders could, with cunning play, defeat the contracts. Imagine that these are all the first games in a rubber, so no-one is vulnerable.

Example 1

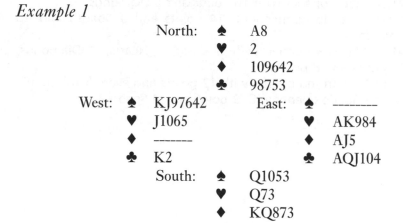

	North:	♠	A8
		♥	2
		♦	109642
		♣	98753

West: ♠ KJ97642   East: ♠ ‒‒‒‒‒‒‒‒
     ♥ J1065   ♥ AK984
     ♦ ‒‒‒‒‒‒‒   ♦ AJ5
     ♣ K2   ♣ AQJ104

         South: ♠ Q1053
              ♥ Q73
              ♦ KQ873
              ♣ 6

West opens the bidding with '3 Spades' (a pre-emptive bid 6-10 points) and only 6 Losers.
North says 'No Bid'.

East, with 19 points, is strong enough to change the suit and bids the higher of her two 5 card suits '4 Hearts'.

South says 'No Bid'.

West knowing her partner has at least 16 points and approving of the Hearts, bids '4 No Trumps' (Blackwood).

North still cannot bid.

East, replies '5 Spades' (meaning 3 Aces).

South says 'No Bid'.

West, realising that they now have to go to 6 in order to return to their Hearts, thinks that she might as well find out whether her partner does hold the two Kings that she is missing, because the answer will only be 6 Clubs (0 Aces), 6 Diamonds (1 Ace) or 6 Hearts (2 Aces), so says '5 No Trumps'.

North once again repeats his 'No Bid'.

East replies '6 Diamonds' (1 King).

South says 'No Bid'.

West, knowing that they are lacking one Ace and one King, must now return to their suit and bid '6 Hearts'.

North and East say 'No Bid'.

South, with only 6 Losers, three trumps including the Queen, and the King and Queen of Diamonds, says 'Double'.

The bidding ends there. The Contract is 6 Hearts Doubled played by East.

South leads his King of Diamonds (top of Honours), which is trumped by Dummy's 5 Hearts.

Dummy (West) leads the Jack of Hearts (top of touching Honours) to try and extract the missing Queen while East has the King and Ace sitting over it. However, North puts on his 2 Hearts and East throws her 4 Hearts, in case North might have been holding on to the Queen, but, no joy, South triumphantly plays her Queen.

South now leads his singleton Club. Dummy puts on 2 Clubs, North his 8 Clubs and it is won by East's 10 Clubs.

East leads her Jack of Diamonds to Dummy's 6 Hearts.

Dummy plays her 10 Hearts. North throws a small Club. East overtakes her partner with the Ace of trumps, so that she can lead from her hand and get out South's lone trump.

East plays her King of Hearts and South's 7 Hearts falls.

East now plays her 4 Clubs to Dummy's King Clubs.

Dummy leads back a small Spade which is taken by North's Ace and then trumped by East.

East is now in the happy position of being able to play out her winning Clubs, her Ace of Diamonds and then her last trump.

6 Hearts Doubled bid and made, which is a tremendous score for East and West. They get 360 points below the line, 50 for the insult and 500 for the Small Slam.

Example 2

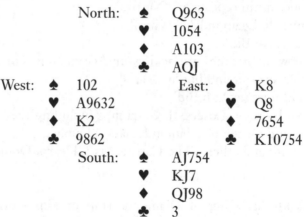

		North:	♠	Q963
			♥	1054
			♦	A103
			♣	AQJ

West:	♠	102	East:	♠	K8
	♥	A9632		♥	Q8
	♦	K2		♦	7654
	♣	9862		♣	K10754

		South:	♠	AJ754
			♥	KJ7
			♦	QJ98
			♣	3

North opens the bidding with '1 No Trump', having 13 points and 8 Losing Tricks.

East says 'No Bid'.

South, with 12 points and 7 Losers, does a Strong Weakness Take-Out and jumps to '3 Spades'.

West says 'No Bid'.

North, with 4 Spades, bids a game, '4 Spades'.

The contract is 4 Spades played by South.

West leads the Ace of Hearts and then continues with the 2 Hearts taken by South's King of Hearts, East's Queen of Hearts falling, leaving South's Jack of Hearts as a potential winner in that suit.

South, knowing that the King of Diamonds is in one of his

opponent's hands, now plays the Queen of Diamonds, trying to extract the King so that he can overtake that with Dummy's Ace of Diamonds. West ducks it and plays her 2 Diamonds, so Dummy also ducks and puts on his 3 Diamonds.

Now, realizing that the missing King of Diamonds must be in West's hand, South continues with his 8 Diamonds; West's King falls and Dummy's Ace takes the trick.

South has now achieved his object of being able to lead the Queen of Trumps from Dummy's hand and tempt out the King of Spades while the Ace of Spades is in his own hand. East covers the honour playing her King and that, in its turn, is taken by South's Ace. There is always a toss-up between '2nd player plays low' and 'cover an honour with an honour'.

South follows on with his Jack of Spades and both West and East follow suit, so South knows that there are no more trumps out against him.

He leads the Jack of Diamonds and then his last remaining Diamond, the 9, throwing his Jack of Clubs from Dummy. He plays the 3 Clubs to his Ace of Clubs, and then the 10 Hearts from Dummy's hand to his own Jack of Hearts.

Only trumps remain. Six Spades have been made, but it was only through successful finessing and it would have been very difficult to bid higher than the game.

Four Spades successfully won.

North/South score 120 below the line and 60 above the line.

Example 3

	North:	♠	KJ10832
		♥	96
		♦	A43
		♣	AJ

West:	♠	Q95	East:	♠	A6
	♥	107		♥	KQJ53
	♦	97652		♦	KJ108
	♣	1053		♣	Q4

	South:	♠	74
		♥	A842
		♦	Q
		♣	K98762

North opens the bidding with '1 Spade'.

East with 16 points overcalls and says '1 No Trump', she could have bid 3 Hearts (a jump shift), but keeps the bidding lower this way (try not to use up 'bidding space' by going so high that you are unable to find a 'fit' with your partner at a lower level).

South with 9 points and 7 Losers bids '2 Clubs'.

West supports her partner with a weakness take-out and bids '2 Diamonds'.

North, as he has six, now rebids his Spades saying '2 Spades'.

East, with four of her partner's Diamonds, bids '3 Diamonds'.

South says 'No Bid'.

West passes.

North, knowing that their opponents have been bidding and that East has at least 16 points, merely bids '3 Spades'. East also says 'No Bid'. The Contract is 3 Spades played by North. You cannot, obviously, always bid a game, particularly if everyone has been bidding.

East plays the Jack of Diamonds (top of touching Honours) taken by Dummy's singleton Queen of Diamonds.

Dummy now plays his 2 Clubs (bottom to an Honour) and West puts on 3 Clubs and North takes the trick with the Ace of Clubs.

Because North is missing the Ace and Queen of trumps, he wants to get into Dummy to play his small trumps and try to trap those two missing honours.

So he plays back the Jack of Clubs and East has to put on the Queen of Clubs and South wins with the King of Clubs.

North now plays the 7 Spades (top of doubleton) from his Dummy and West puts on her 5 Spades, North plays his Jack of Spades and it is taken by East's Ace of Spades, making North realise that West must have the Queen of Spades or North would have played it rather than the Ace. North is happy because his King of Spades is now sitting over West's Queen.

East plays her King of Hearts and Dummy, West and North throw small Hearts. East continues with her Queen of Hearts, but this time it is overtaken by Dummy's Ace of Hearts.

The 4 Spades is played from Dummy, West putting on her 9 Spades and North overtaking it with the 10 Spades. Then, knowing that there is only Queen of trumps outstanding, North plays his King of Spades, successfully taking West's Queen, East throwing her 3 Hearts.

North then plays his Ace of Diamonds, throwing a low Club from Dummy.

North plays out the 8 of trumps, East throws the 5 Clubs and West a low Diamond. North surrenders and plays the 9 Hearts taken by East's Jack of Hearts and East then leads her King of Diamonds and North is unable to trump it. However, East's lead of 10 Diamonds is, of course, trumped by North's last trump. 3 Spades bid and won.

23

Etiquette

You already know about choosing your partner, where to sit, and how to shuffle and deal the cards. Now that you can, I hope, really enjoy your Bridge and are relaxed, here are just a few hints about the way that you need to behave at the table.

Never gloat or look smug. This is even more unpleasant than the player who grumbles that he never gets any cards.

If you are the dummy, it is not considered polite to get up and wander around the table peering at the other people's cards. Sometimes, of course, in a friendly game, the declarer might ask her opponents whether she could pass her cards across to the dummy so that her bidding and playing can be explained at the end of that particular game.

Although chatting and laughing should be encouraged, it is not polite to start a conversation just as the cards have been dealt or when someone is having trouble playing a game. Try and keep your interesting talk for the periods in between the hands, or during the times when you are not actually at the table.

Never vary the intonation in your bidding. Never put a question mark in your voice at the end of your bid to make sure that your partner realises that your '4 No Trump' bid was Blackwood!

Long pauses before bidding are to be avoided. For example, a pause followed by 'no bid' tells everyone that you have not quite enough points to open. Equally, opening the bidding immediately you have looked at your cards and saying 'No Bid' could well tell everyone that you have seen at a glance that you have very few High Card Points. It is incredibly bad manners to open the bidding immediately you have your cards anyway, because some people sort their cards much more slowly and will feel pressured and intimidated; on the other hand try not to be too slow, because you might irritate another player.

Play your cards at the same speed. Fumbling or hesitating before you play a card on a trick means that your opponents may realise that you hold that all important missing card and they will take the appropriate action.

Be careful about holding your cards close to you, by 'chesting them'. It is very irritating when you can see your opponent's cards and have to keep trying to play looking everywhere except in her direction.

Use the proper language. It is better to say 'No Bid' rather than 'Pass', which might sound like 'Hearts'. Say 'Double' not 'I'll double 4 Hearts', which sounds as if you wouldn't double anything else.

One of the most important things about playing Bridge is finding out the conventions, however simply you want to play, that are used by your partner and the opponents. This is done at the very beginning when you first sit down. Not only must you listen to your partner, you must also hear and understand what your opponents are aiming to do. If they say some extraordinary convention that you have never heard about, ask them what they mean. I know that when you are playing friendly social Bridge, you can always ask when the actual moment arises; but, if you are in a competition or playing in a Club, they will frown upon extraneous conversation and expect you to have found everything out beforehand. However, supposing one of your opponents makes a bid during the game that seems incomprehensible, it is perfectly permissible to ask their partner "What do you understand by your partner's bid?".

Remember that the bidding system is not some secret between you and your partner. Your opponents are entitled to know as much about what your bidding means as your partner.

Always thank your dummy when their cards are laid down, even if they are not quite what you expected! Say at the end of the game "That was fun". If your partner has not played particularly well, you could say "Bad Luck" and leave it at that.

Be generous and kind always.

Bridge gets a bad press because some partners criticise each other or try and tell their opponents what they should have done. If anyone wants some advice about their bidding or play at the end of a particular hand, leave it to them to ask.

Never try and 'teach' anyone unsolicited at the table. You are aiming to be a popular player, one that everyone wants to be their partner. Post-mortems can be constructive, but it is preferable to keep all of them until after the whole session is over; or, even more sensibly, forgive and forget and just make another date for the 'next time'.

24

Parties, Chicago, Two and Three-Handed Bridge

Many organisations already fund-raise by holding Bridge parties. These can be a lucrative and fairly easy way of making money. They can be whole day events where a buffet is laid out and, at a certain stage in the proceedings, people are invited to come up table by table and help themselves. If it is a tea-time occasion it is important to offer a good selection of sandwiches and cakes; also to make certain that there is enough tea for everyone, and coffee for those who prefer it.

For a buffet meal, salads are generally the best option, or in the winter something like lasagnes or cottage pie which can be dished out in large amounts. People are often keen to help, even if they are not on the Committee and I have done some successful Bridge parties for a fairly large number by asking everyone to bring something, making certain that there is not too much of some particular food, or lacking something else which would be missed. However, always remember to check any current regulations regarding food.

Quite often ordinary Rubber Bridge is played and every table is asked to play a certain number of hands, dependent on the time allotted. To make the event more interesting, the compere, or organiser, could announce "for your next hand, irrespective of what is dealt, North/South will play 3 No Trumps doubled" or "6 Hearts redoubled". The whole point is for everyone to have fun and, if you want to give prizes it could be for the biggest score for each North/South and each East/West, or perhaps for the first couple to bid and win a Slam.

113

Sometimes everyone is told that after each four hands North/South should move to the next table. This means that different people play together.

Chicago

This can be quite fun. Partners stay together and play four hands and then the losing pair at each table move to the next table up and the winners stay where they are and get ready to play with the losers from the table before. Everyone must wait to start at their new table until all are in position. For the first hand at each table no-one is vulnerable; for the second hand the dealer and her partner are vulnerable; the third hand the new dealer and partner are vulnerable; and for the 4th hand everyone is vulnerable. Each hand is completely separate and a part-score cannot be carried forward to the next hand.

The scoring is exactly the same as for Rubber Bridge with the added incentive that if you win your contract with a part-score you get an extra 50 points; for example if you bid and made 2 Hearts you would score 60 + 50 = 110 points. If you bid and win a game and you are non-vulnerable you score an extra 300 points and if vulnerable an extra 500 points. There is no above and below the line, all the points are put down together on the score sheet. On the whole you will find that Chicago players seem to 'bid up' more than the safer Rubber players, because they are anxious to gain the extra points for a successful contract, particularly to make a game. Slam points and Doubling count for exactly the same as in Rubber Bridge; however Honours are not counted. Obviously, the pair scoring the highest at the end of the tournament are the winners.

There are some social players who play Chicago even if they only have one table. After each four hands, everyone moves around and plays with a different person, and then again until they have all played with a new partner.

Sometimes you feel like playing Bridge, but don't have a foursome. The Two, and Three-Handed variations are fun and also an extremely good way to continue to work at your increasing knowledge of the game.

Three-Handed Bridge
I used to play this with my mother and my brother, who started when he was only three, because my father refused to take up such a 'time-wasting game'. I think, in fact I am sure, that it was his loss! I am not certain where my mother picked up this game or whether she designed it herself, but it was a rival for our attention together with Racing Demon, Poker Patience and Vingt-et-un.

Having drawn for deal, four hands of twelve cards each are dealt. The other four cards are to be handed to the winner of the contract. The three players sort out their hands, leaving dummy face down on the table.

As is usual, the dealer starts the bidding. The one who wins the final contract is now able to turn up her dummy, and then she hands out one of each of the four extra cards face down to every player, including dummy and herself. Play and scoring now continues as normal.

This is, obviously, not as good as proper Rubber Bridge with four players, because, as everyone is playing independently, you miss the interaction between yourself and your partner, not just with the bidding, but also with the play. However, if someone lets you down and you are left with just a threesome, this can keep your guests fairly happy!

Two-Handed or Honeymoon Bridge

The name "Honeymoon Bridge" can be applied to any adaptation of Contract Bridge for two players. There are several versions and all of them use a 52-card pack, with suits and cards in each suit ranking as in Bridge. Scoring is the same as in Rubber Bridge.

Draw Bridge

The dealer shuffles and dealer's opponent cuts. The dealer deals 13 cards to each player, one at a time. The remaining 26 cards are placed face down to form a stock.

The first 13 tricks are played as No Trumps. Non-dealer leads to the first trick, and it is not necessary to follow suit. These tricks do not count towards the score – they are simply discarded – but the winner of each trick draws the top card from the top of the stock and the loser takes the next card. When drawing a card you add it to your hand without showing it to your opponent.

After 13 tricks each player still has 13 cards, and if they have very good memories they will know each other's hands. The players now bid as in Contract Bridge (double and redoubles are allowed), until one player passes. The final contract is then played – the opponent of the bidder leading to the first trick. Suit must be followed as in Bridge.

There are variations: some players turn the top card of the stock face up before the lead to each trick, so in the first 13 tricks you know what card you will pick up if you win the trick – but not if you lose. Another variation is that you have to follow suit in the first 13 tricks. However, since following suit is not enforceable when players draw new cards after each trick, it is probably better to play that you don't have to. In the last 13 tricks suit must always be followed as in Bridge.

Draw And Discard Bridge
No cards are dealt, but after shuffling and cutting, the 52 cards are stacked face down. The players take turns to draw cards as follows: at your turn you look at the top card of the stock without showing it to your opponent; you may either take this card and add it to your hand, or discard it to a face down discard pile. If you reject the first stock card you *must* take the next stock card and add it to the hand. If you take the first stock card you look at the next stock card and *must* discard it face down. Players take alternate turns until the stock is exhausted. At this time, each player has a hand of 13 cards, and has seen 13 of the 26 cards in the discard pile, but does not know which of the other 26 cards are in the opponent's hand.

The players now bid as in Contract Bridge (doubles and redoubles are allowed), until one player passes. The final contract is then played, the opponent of the bidder leading to the first trick. Suit must be followed as in Bridge.

A variation of this is that in drawing, a player who accepts the top card of the stock does not look at and discard the next card. In this version, there will generally be some stock cards left over when each player has collected their 13 cards. Neither player knows what these remaining stock cards are.

Double Dummy Bridge

The two active players sit next to each other. Four 13-card hands are dealt as in Contract Bridge – a hand for each player and two dummy hands. The hand opposite each player is their dummy, but they cannot look at it until after the bidding.

The two players bid as in Contract Bridge (doubles and redoubles allowed) until one player passes. The players then look at their own dummies, but not to show them to each other until after the opening lead.

The declarer's opponent leads a card to the first trick from the hand that will be to declarer's left: this will be the opponent's own hand if the declarer is the right-hand player, but the opponent's dummy if the declarer is the left-hand player. Both dummies are then exposed on the table, opposite their owners, and play continues as in Bridge, each of the players playing cards from their own dummy in its turn.

To eliminate any positional advantage in sitting to the left or right, there is a variation where some play that the hands are always arranged, after the bidding, in clockwise order: opponent's dummy, declarer's dummy, opponent, declarer. In this case the opponent's dummy leads to the first trick.

Some deal just 12 cards to each player initially. Players may look at their own dummies during the bidding. After the bidding, the dealer deals two more cards to each player. The players look at the extra cards and choose which to add to their own hand and which to their dummy.

Single Dummy Bridge

Four hands are dealt as in Double Dummy Bridge, but one hand is exposed before the bidding. After the bidding, the declarer chooses whether to have the exposed dummy as a partner. Either way, the second dummy is then exposed and the play continues as in Double Dummy Bridge.

Bridge With Semi-Exposed Dummies

The players sit next to each other. Four 13-card hands are dealt. The hands belonging to the players are dealt normally, but each of the dummies are arranged with six cards face up at the end of the row with no card under it. Each active player owns and plays the dummy opposite them.

The two players bid as at Contract Bridge (doubles and redoubles allowed) until one player passes. In this version each player can of course see seven cards of each dummy as well as their own cards during the bidding. The hand to the declarer's left leads to the first trick. When it is the turn of a dummy hand to play, its owner plays a face up card from it, obeying the usual rules of following suit. If this exposes a face down card, that card is turned face up at the end of the trick.

Memory Bridge

13 cards are dealt to each player and played as a No Trump. Suit must be followed, and there is no drawing of replacement cards as in Draw Bridge. The player who makes seven or more tricks scores as though they had played a contract of 1 NT, and get an additional premium of 100 above the line.

The remaining cards are then dealt, 13 to each player, and bid, played and scored as in Bridge.

25

Postscript

My aim in writing this book has been to keep everything as simple as possible. However, Bridge teaching varies from region to region and teacher to teacher, although I have tried to stick as closely as possible to the Acol Bridge system.

With bridge beginners I teach that opening with 1 No Trump is 12 -15; and a 1 No Trump reply is 6 to _10_ points; a 2 No Trump reply is _11_ to 12; and an overcall with 1 No Trump is 16-17 points, and 2 No Trumps is 18-19 points. I have also written in this book that with two five card suits you bid the higher ranking first, and with two four card suits you bid the lower ranking. Acol Bridge players always bid the higher of the two suits irrespective of whether they are 4 or 5 card ones. In my opinion I find that it is extremely useful to be able to work out that if a Heart has been bid by my partner and then on his second bid he says a Diamond – I _know_ that he has 5 Hearts and he may have 4 or 5 Diamonds; and that if he bids a Diamond followed by a Heart – his Diamonds may be a 4 or 5 card suit and his Heart suit will be a 4 card one.

Now that you CAN play, you may find that you might like to change your configuration a little and bid in a slightly different way. Remember that Bridge is a game with no absolutes as it is constantly evolving. Some of the best players play 'by the seat of their pants' but, of course, they have learned some basic principles and adapted them to their own needs.

Most players in Britain play using the weak No Trump, although many older players and those who have lived or are living abroad use a strong No Trump – if you come up against this, just explain that you like to "play weak".

Remember the aim is to *enjoy* the game! There are, of course, some 'contraptions' that would actually add to your pleasure but try and play like this – simply and well. Perhaps, if you feel adventurous, and when you are really confident, I suggest you look for the sequel to this book, which will explain such fascinating 'contraptions' as the 'Strong No Trump' and the 'Phoney Club', 'Stayman', 'Transfers', 'Weak Two's', 'Benjamin Two's', 'Roman Key Blackwood' and 'Cue Bidding'.

Some of you may quite possibly feel that you want to join a Club and play at a higher standard. Do! But please, if you also continue to play Rubber Bridge socially, don't expect these players to wish to play at the same speed, or with lots of conventions. Sometimes, my pupils have complained about one or other of their number who starts criticising and makes bridge uncomfortable. If you ever feel that you are becoming guilty in this way, please try to be kinder.

Good luck to all of you in your future play.

26

I thought this might be of interest to you, now that you are <u>real</u> Bridge players!

A Brief History of Bridge
by Jonathan Goodall

The first formal rules of Bridge were drawn up in 1895 by the card committee of the Portland Club in London. It had been introduced the year before by Lord Brougham on his return from a visit to Cairo where he had found it being played. Its origins, though, can be traced back to 1482 in France to the game of Triumph, which by the end of the 16th century had become in England 'a verie common alehouse game'. During the course of the next 100 years similar, or synonymous, games such as Ruff-and-Honours, Trump, Slamm and Whisk emerged; all, as their names suggest, containing elements of the game played to-day. By the first quarter of the 18th century these had evolved into the single game of Whist which by then had become respectable, moving up in the world from the alehouse to the coffee house. The first authoritative treatment of the game appeared in 1742 when Edmond Hoyle published his *Short Treatise on the Game of Whist*, and in 1760 White's Chocolate House was the first gaming establishment formally to adopt a set of rules.

Quite how, where or when Bridge evolved from Whist is uncertain. The common explanation is that it originated in Russia. But this is based upon the existence of a pamphlet circulating in London in 1886 entitled *Biritch or Russian Whist* in which the dealer declared trumps after dummy's hand was exposed. However, there was nothing new in either choosing trumps or playing the dummy. In the 1700s a certain Bishop of Winchester was renowned for choosing trumps from his own hand when playing with his compliant chaplains, and Dummy Whist for three players had been played in social circles for the best part of a century. The earliest reference to Bridge as a game is to be found in a letter of 1843 from a Dr. Paget to his fiancée in which the writer mentions passing the time in the 'intellectual games of Bagatelle and Bridge'. If the game of Bridge that he refers to was indeed a card game it is perfectly possible that it was a version of Dummy Whist in which the two hands were 'bridged' for the purpose of selecting trumps and playing the hand. The word 'Biritch' is almost certainly a corruption of the word 'Bridge', and if such a game were played in England in the 1840s the most likely explanation is that it was picked up by the Russians, perhaps from their prisoners, during the Crimean War.

The game of 1895 was much the same as that of today except that the scoring levels were different and there was no bidding. In Whist, trumps were determined by the dealer turning up the last card dealt, but in Bridge the dealer had the option of choosing trumps, or none, after inspecting his hand, or of passing the decision to his partner who was then obliged to make a declaration. The opponents could then double the value of the tricks if either of them thought they could make more tricks than the dealer, but the trump suit was fixed. The fundamental problem was that the black suits were undervalued. Spades were at that time the lowest suit at 2 points per trick with Clubs at 4 points; Diamonds, Hearts and No Trumps were worth 6, 8 and 12 points respectively. Game was 30 points which made it impossible to score game with Spades as trumps, even if doubled. Hence the expression to do something 'in spades'. Since this impossibility applied equally to either side the dealer tended to declare Spades as trumps whenever he held a worthless hand, almost irrespective of his holding in that suit, purely to make it impossible for the opponents to score game. This frequently resulted in the dealer playing out pointless hands that rightly belonged to the other side.

The introduction of Auction Bridge by the Bath and Portland Clubs jointly in 1908 allowed each player in turn to bid for the right to play the hand and choose the declaration. But it suffered from the defect that it was trick value rather than the ranking of the suits that governed the bidding. The rules did not allow the dealer to pass: if his hand was remotely suitable he bid 1 No Trump as it offered the shortest route to game. In theory, an opponent holding Spades then had to bid 7 Spades in order to overcall. The effect was to cut the black suits out of the game.

The American solution in 1911 was Royal Auction Bridge which introduced a new suit called 'Royals' (in actuality the Spade suit) between Hearts and No Trumps. The trick values were revised to 6, 7, 8, 9 and 10 for Clubs through to No Trumps with the dual purpose Spade suit retaining its value of 2 points per trick. This enabled the dealer to open the bidding, as he was still obliged to do, with 1 Spade on a worthless hand.

In 1914 the Portland Club, which preferred to 'call a spade a spade', abolished Royals along with the lower value for the Spade suit and allowed the dealer to pass. At about that time value bidding gave way to majority bidding in America but persisted in England until 1928. It was the final stage in the evolution of Auction Bridge and, as with all the rule changes, was the formal confirmation of common practice.

Throughout all these developments the basic principle of Whist, that points won in winning tricks scored towards game, was retained – provided the number of tricks taken was at least equal to the bid. There was no requirement to bid game in order to score game. Nevertheless, by the mid 1920s bidding had become so competitive that being held to a contract was a change waiting to happen.

It is a common misconception that Contract Bridge was 'invented' in America by Harold Vanderbilt in the closing months of 1925. In fact, the contract principle was being experimented with virtually everywhere else, but mainly in Europe, as early as 1912. The first known set of rules, published by Sir Hugh Clayton in *The Times of India* newspaper in 1914, did not allow overtricks to be scored at all unless doubled, and increased by bonuses for Small and Grand Slams tenfold to 500 and 1000 points respectively. By 1918 a version called Plafond ('ceiling') was being played in France, but overtricks scored 50 points each, plus a 50 point bonus for fulfilling the contract, with under-tricks penalised at 100 points each. As Auction trick values applied (10 points at the most) there was every incentive to underbid, with the result that rubbers tended to become inordinately long. A better game existed concurrently in Canada, devised by G. H. Levy, in which overtricks scored only 10 points each and there was a sliding scale for penalties. Slam bonuses were also raised to 250 and 500 points respectively.

In the year 1920 three books were published in England with the word 'Contract' in their title and in 1926 *Contract Bridge* by E. Monteith was published, also in England, which included 'the American and one Continental' scoring table. The former was essentially Plafond, but that of the Berlin Sports Club incorporated what we now call vulnerability in which both penalties and overtricks were doubled in the rubber game. No doubt it featured elsewhere on the Continent but not apparently in America at that time.

Harold Vanderbilt's true contribution was to bring together a unified, balanced scoring table which has changed little since. His only real innovation was to raise the game score from 30 points to 100 points and to increase the trick values accordingly. The Whist Club of New York officially adopted the new scoring and issued the first rules of Contract Bridge as we know it today in September 1927. This was followed in January 1929 by the Portland Club in London, just 34 years after it drew up the very first official rules of Bridge in 1895.

Reference: *The Golden Age of Contract Bridge* by David Daniels, 1982.

Having read this, I should think that you are breathing a sigh of relief that you don't have to play some of the even more complicated games that preceded the wonderful game that is now *your* Bridge.
C.S.

27
RECIPES

Having people to your house to play Bridge doesn't mean that you must work hard in the kitchen beforehand. A cup of tea or coffee and some bought biscuits or cakes are sometimes quite enough; after all, having to stop for a meal does detract from the time you can spend at the card table! However, if you feel like actually feeding your guests, here are some ideas to get you going.

CONTENTS

SOUPS

Bridge is an extremely social game. Tea is an easy meal, but lunch can be equally carefree; remember your guests regard the food, however delicious, as a pause before the real event.

Sometimes, of course, lunch can be a more formal meal and you may, then, start with soup and then continue with one of the main course recipes; or, simply, go from soup to a pudding.

If you have invited people to lunch and Bridge, generally you eat first and then turn to the cards. If it is an evening event, many people choose to play a rubber before the meal and then continue afterwards. Bridge is so flexible and so rewarding: even if *you* don't win, someone at the table will go home feeling happier and pleased with themselves!

SOUP

After a lot of experience, many of my fellow players and I have come to the conclusion that soup is the best answer for lunch, if you are going to have a jolly afternoon playing Bridge without people nodding off.

In winter there is nothing as warming as a bowl of steaming soup served with delicious bread and, perhaps, some cheese and fruit. In summer cold soup is refreshing. Nowadays, it is easy to buy really good soup and enhance it with various things such as croutons, cubes of an appropriate vegetable, cooked if necessary, sherry, a squeeze of lemon juice, some curry powder, and cream or fromage frais.

Making your own soup is not very arduous and gives you a certain kudos! Real stock makes a tremendous difference. Whenever I have a chicken I put the carcass in a casserole in the oven and cook it slowly until it looks as if it is going to jellify. I have a stack of pots of stock in the freezer all ready to defrost and then I can add whatever vegetables are in season. I always put in an apple, and quite often orange juice. If, however, you have no stock, bought stock cubes can work very well!

I would suggest: Pea; mushroom; courgette or marrow with cream cheese (sometimes with a herby cream cheese); vegetable; potato and leak; Stilton and Guinness; tomato, and, of course the special soups that I have included in this book.

SOUPE VERTE

50g./2oz. butter
110g./4oz. onion, finely chopped
225g./8oz. potatoes, peeled and chopped
1 bunch of watercress, coarsely chopped
1/2 cucumber (about 225gm./8oz. peeled and diced)
The outside leaves of a lettuce (about 110g./4oz) shredded
1 level tablespoon flour
110g./4oz. frozen peas
425ml./^{3}/4pt. stock (or water plus 1 chicken stock cube)
425ml./^{3}/4pt. milk
Salt and pepper
65ml./2^1/2fl.oz. fresh single cream

Serves 4 very comfortably, probably with some left over.

1. Melt the butter in a saucepan and fry the onion and potatoes gently until softening but not coloured; stir from time to time. Add the watercress, cucumber and shredded lettuce and fry very gently for a further 5 minutes, turning frequently.
2. Sprinkle the slightly cooked vegetables with the flour. Cook for a further minute then add the peas and mix in the stock. Simmer for about 30 minutes.
3. Puree the soup, add the milk and return to the saucepan. Season the soup to taste, bring slowly to the boil then remove the pan from the heat to cool slightly before stirring in the cream.

Cook's comment: This is a pretty soup with a delicate summer flavour. It can be served either hot or cold for a light lunch, perhaps followed by a cheeseboard and grapes.

CREAM OF SPINACH SOUP

275ml./^{1}/₂pt. milk   50g./2oz. onion, chopped
3 cloves   1 blade of mace
3 peppercorns   350g./12oz. fresh spinach
2 chicken stock cubes dissolved in 1 pint of water
(or 570ml./1pt. home-made chicken stock)
25g./1oz. flour
25g./1oz. butter
Salt and pepper, grated nutmeg
65ml./2^1/₂ fl.oz. fresh single cream

Serves 4, generously.

1. Very gently heat the milk for 10 minutes together with the onion, cloves, mace and peppercorns. Leave until cold then strain.
2. Cook the fresh spinach in 570ml./1pt. water with the stock cubes (or, alternatively, cook in the home-made stock) for about 10-15 minutes or until it is very tender, then liquidise and place aside.
3. Combine the butter, flour and milk in a large heavy saucepan over a medium heat. Whisk briskly with a balloon whisk until the sauce is thick.
4. Remove the pan from the heat and blend in the spinach puree.
5. Stirring continuously, bring the soup to the boil then simmer gently for 5 minutes. Cool slightly then season to taste with salt, pepper and grated nutmeg. Stir in all but 2 tablespoons of the cream.
6. Ladle the soup into bowls and swirl a little cream in each to serve.

Cook's comment: Fresh spinach can be replaced with a 250g./9oz. packet of frozen spinach. Some boiling sausage or sliced frankfurters would add flavour.

French bread and butter is an essential accompaniment.

WILD MUSHROOM SOUP
WITH CROUTONS

350g./12oz. wild or field mushrooms
1 medium potato peeled and cut into 1cm sq pieces
1 large onion
1 clove garlic
25g./1oz butter
1 tablespoon olive oil
570ml./1pt light stock (or 2 chicken or vegetable stock cubes
dissolved in 1pt water)
275ml./$^1/_2$ pint milk
Pinch of paprika
Salt and pepper to taste
50g./2oz. Parmesan flakes
4 dessertspoonfuls single cream to serve

Serves 4

1. Peel and chop onion and garlic.
2. Wash, dry and roughly chop mushrooms (if field mushrooms, slice each in half and check carefully).
3. Melt butter and olive oil together on low heat.
4. Add onion and garlic, cover pan and leave until soft and translucent.
5. Add potato, increase heat slightly and sauté for 5 minutes.
6. Add mushrooms and paprika, cook for a further 5 minutes, then add stock.
7. Bring to simmering point and cook gently for about 20 minutes, checking that the potato is soft.
8. Pour into a blender and blend until smooth.
9. Strain into a bowl, then add warmed milk and return to pan.
10. Adjust the seasoning.
11. Serve with a few flakes of parmesan and a swirl of cream.

CROUTONS

4 thick slices of bread (brown, white or granary to taste) cut into 1 cm cubes
125ml/4 oz. olive oil

1. Heat olive oil in frying pan until hot enough to fry a cube of bread in a few seconds.
2. Add cubed bread and keep turning in hot oil until all sides are a pale golden brown.
3. Drain on a paper towel and serve immediately with the soup.

Hungarian Beef Soup
with Pickled Cucumber and Soured Cream

110g./4oz. onion, chopped   225g./8oz. minced beef
25gm./1oz. butter   225g./8oz. tin tomatoes
850ml./1¹/₂pts. stock (or 3 chicken stock cubes dissolved in
1¹/₂ pints water)
Salt and pepper
2 cloves of garlic, crushed
3 or 4 pickled cucumber, sliced
4 tablespoons of soured cream

This nourishing soup will serve 6-8 people, but you can always keep some for yourself for the next day, as long as the remainder is put into the refrigerator when it is cool and then heated up properly once again.

1. Fry the chopped onion and minced beef in the butter until lightly browned.
2. Add the diced potato and fry for a further 2-3 minutes.
3. Stir in the tinned tomatoes with their juice, the stock, salt, pepper and garlic. Simmer gently for 30 minutes, then add the sliced pickled cucumbers.
4. Ladle the soup into bowls and swirl in the soured cream.

Cook's comment: A heart-warming winter soup that is a meal in itself. Tinned broad or butter beans may be added and dumplings too, if you want to make it even more substantial. The cucumber and soured cream really make it, so don't be tempted to leave them out.

French bread and butter is an essential accompaniment.

Minestrone Soup

225g./8oz. tin of tomatoes
2 tablespoons of tomato puree
2 carrots, diced   1 parsnip, diced
110g./4oz. frozen peas
1 onion chopped finely
1 clove of garlic, crushed (optional)
570ml./1pt. home-made stock, or 1 pt. water with
2 chicken stock cubes
Salt and pepper   1 bay leaf
40g./1$^{1}/_{2}$oz. macaroni
50g./2oz. Cheddar cheese grated

Serves 4–6

1. Pour the stock (or water and stock cubes) into a large saucepan.
2. To this add the carrots, parsnip, onion, garlic (if using), the tin of tomatoes, the tomato puree, salt and pepper and the bay leaf.
3. Bring to the boil and simmer until the vegetables are soft, but still firm.
4. While the saucepan is still simmering, add the macaroni and cook until it is al dente. Then add the frozen peas and continue to cook for 3–4 minutes.
5. The soup can be poured into bowls and the cheese passed around to be spooned on top.

Cook's comment: You can always add a drop of sherry just before the soup is served, and any other vegetables that you might have in the larder, like courgettes or finely chopped and de-stringed celery.

If you would prefer this soup as a cream one, simply omit the macaroni and take out the bay leaf, allow to cool and then liquidise, adding some cream before serving and probably don't have the separate bowl of grated cheese.

LUNCHES OR SUPPERS

Sometimes soups are not really what you feel like cooking, or you have given the same people soup before; in which case, look through the recipes and find something else to tempt your future partner and, of course, your opponents.

COLD

ITALIAN MEAT SALAD

25g./1oz. fresh parsley, finely chopped
25g./1oz. spring onions, finely chopped
1 clove of garlic, finely chopped or crushed (optional)
2 medium sized tomatoes, peeled
1 tablespoon of capers, finely chopped
4 tablespoons of fresh white breadcrumbs
8 tablespoons of oil
4 tablespoons of lemon juice   Salt and pepper
350g./12oz. very thinly sliced cold roast or boiled meat (port, chicken, veal or beef are best)
Watercress to garnish

Serves 4–6

1. Place the chopped parsley, spring onions and garlic in a bowl.
2. Finely chop the tomatoes and add them to the chopped capers.
3. Stir in the breadcrumbs, oil, lemon juice, salt and pepper.
4. Arrange the meat in a layer on a large flat plate and spoon the sauce over; cover and leave in a cool place for at least an hour.
5. Swirl the cream over the dressing just before serving the meat salad.

Cook's comment: A particularly salad and a great way to use up cold roast meat. Good with warmed potato salad and dressed chicory.

CREAMED EGGS WITH A BLACK HAT

6 hard-boiled eggs
75g./3oz. melted butter
75g./3oz. Philadelphia Soft Cheese Light
75g./3oz. double cream
Salt and pepper
Small tin of mock caviar – preferably black

Serves 4

1. When the eggs are cool chop them up into small pieces and add the melted butter to bind them.
2. Put this mixture onto a plate, spread into a round and put into the fridge to set.
3. Mix the double cream and the Philadelphia, making certain that it is thick enough to spread and not run off the plate, and spread on top of the egg mixture.
4. At the last minute open the tin of caviar and spread over the eggs.

Cook's comment: Delicious and very rich. A green or tomato salad with a little dressing accompanies this very well.

TOSSED-TOGETHER SALAD

1/2 roast chicken, skinned, de-boned and chopped
3 slices of Parma ham, chopped
1 head of chicory
1 small crisp lettuce
2 sticks of celery, chopped
2 hard-boiled eggs
12 small tomatoes, left whole
125g./4oz. French beans, cooked but *al dente*
1 crisp red eating apple, sliced finely with the skin left on
and kept covered with some vinaigrette
175g./6oz. small potatoes, cooked and then skinned and cut
in half
50g./2oz. green grapes, un-stoned
A really good home-made French vinaigrette

For the vinaigrette:
1 teaspoon coarse mustard
1 teaspoon runny honey or Muscovy brown sugar.
Mix well together:
2 tablespoons of olive oil
1/2 tablespoon of vinegar – wine, cider, or some Balsamic

Serves 4, but obviously can be increased very easily to feed
more people (perhaps 2 tables of Bridge players).

1. Amalgamate all the ingredients in a large bowl.
2. Just before serving add the sliced apple and vinaigrette
   and toss together.

Cook's comment: This is a delicious and very easy meal,
provided you have amassed all the ingredients. You can
obviously add anything else that you like: salmon and prawns
instead of the chicken and Parma ham; olives; crisp bacon;
diced dried apricots; nuts and raisins; cooked peas; avocado.

My Danish Friend's Gravad Laks

1 piece of raw salmon on the bone
2 tablespoons coarse salt   2 tablespoons sugar
Pepper   Fresh Dill

1. With a firm grip, cut the salmon from the bone, sliding along the backbone.
2. Turn the salmon over and repeat with the other side. The ribs attached to the meat are not removed before carving until after it has been cured.
3. Mix the coarse salt and sugar, rubbing into the meaty side. Place in a dish with the skin side underneath.
4. Add fresh pepper and a large amount of freshly cut dill.
5. Repeat with the second side of salmon, placing into the same dish and this time with the skin uppermost.
6. A small piece should be cured for 24 hours, a larger piece for 48 hours.
7. Half way through the curing, drain any liquid that has formed. Turn the piece over.
8. Carve slices as you would carve smoked salmon.

Sauce for Gravad Laks

2 tablespoons vinegar   2 tablespoons Dijon mustard
2 tablespoons sweet mustard   2 tablespoons brown sugar
Oil   Freshly cut dill

Mix vinegar, mustard, sugar and dill. Add the oil as appropriate while mixing.

Marinated Salmon

1. Take any left-over pieces of salmon, cut into thin pieces, put salt on and leave for 30 minutes.
2. Marinate in lemon olive oil.

RAW SALMON WITH MUSTARD AND TOMATO KETCHUP

300g. salmon, fillet or bits
1-2 teaspoons of Dijon mustard
1-2 teaspoons of tomato ketchup
1 tablespoon lemon juice
Salt and pepper
Chives

Serves 4

1. Chop salmon with knife or place briefly in food processor.
2. Add mustard, ketchup, lemon juice, salt and pepper.
3. Divide into 4 portions and decorate with chives.
4. Serve with fresh bread or toast.

HOT FOOD – FISH

POACHED FISH WITH GREEN SAUCE

4 thick portions of skinned fish e.g. cod loin fillets, salmon,
trout etc.
1 level teaspoon of salt
2 parsley stalks
1^1/$_2$ tablespoons of lemon juice
25g./1oz. chopped onion
1 bay leaf
4 peppercorns

For the sauce:
150ml./^{1}/$_4$ pt. fresh double cream, whipped
1^1/$_2$ level tablespoons of parsley, very finely chopped
1 bunch (75g./3oz.) watercress, very finely chopped
2 cocktail gherkins, very finely chopped
^{3}/$_4$ tablespoon of capers
100ml/4fl.oz. mayonnaise
Salt and pepper
Chopped garlic if wanted
Juice of ^{1}/$_2$ lemon
Lemon slices and parsley to garnish

Serves 4

1. Pre-heat a moderate oven 180ºC, Gas Mark 4 – centre shelf.
2. Place the fish in a shallow buttered dish, cover with the
   lemon juice and a little cold water. Add peppercorns,
   parsley stalks, chopped onion, bay leaf and salt.
3. Cover the dish with foil and cook until the fish is just
   tender. Leave to cool in the liquid.
4. Lift the fish out of the liquid and place aside to drain.
5. Place chopped watercress, gherkins, capers and garlic in a
   bowl. Add the mayonnaise, stir together, and fold in the
   whipped cream. Season to taste with salt and pepper and
   lemon juice.

6. Place the drained fish on a serving dish and garnish with lemon slices and parsley. Serve the sauce separately.

Cook's comment: Any fish, either hot or cold, is enhanced by this sharp, well flavoured sauce. Serve with potatoes and a selection of lightly cooked young vegetables. Or, for a light lunch, put the sauce in individual dishes resting on plates and surround each dish with whole prawns for each person to peel and dip in the sauce.

FISH WELLINGTON

4 tablespoons single cream
100g./4oz. chopped mushrooms
25g./1oz. butter
175g./6oz. smooth paté
50g./2oz. onion, finely chopped
salt and pepper
2 large skinned fillets of cod or haddock, approx. 900g./2lb.
375g./14oz. packet puff pastry
Beaten egg

Serves 6-8, but as you will see in Cook's comment, it is very adaptable.

1. Preheat a hot oven 220°C, Gas Mark 7 – upper shelf
2. Fry the chopped mushrooms and onion in the butter until soft. Remove the pan from the heat.
3. Mash the paté in a bowl. Stir in the cream, fried onion and mushrooms. Season to taste with salt and pepper.
4. Roll the pastry to a rectangle 35cm. x 30cm./14in. x 12in.
5. Place one fillet in the centre of the pastry and spread the filling mixture over the fillet. Then top with the other fillet. Trim the pastry round allowing a good 10cm./4in. margin. Reserve this trimmed pastry.
6. Brush round the edges of the pastry with beaten egg and then carefully fold it over the fish and neatly wrap it up like a parcel.
7. Place the parcelled fish on a baking sheet with the sealed edges down. Brush with the beaten egg. Roll pastry trimmings into decorative fish shapes and seal on top of the pastry parcel.
8. Cook in the preheated oven for about 25 minutes until the pastry is golden brown and the fish is cooked through.

Freezer note: Use fresh fish and not pre-frozen puff pastry. This dish may be frozen, uncooked. Store for up to a month. Thaw before cooking.

Cook's comment: Simple to make, this is an impressive looking dish, ideal for a special occasion. It is good served hot with French beans or asparagus, and buttered carrots. Excellent cold too the next day, so don't dish up the whole amount for your Bridge foursome!

FISH PIE

225g./^{1}/$_2$lb. thick haddock (or similar) fillet, skinned
225g./^{1}/$_2$lb. thick salmon fillet, skinned
225g./^{1}/$_2$lb. thick smoked haddock or smoked cod fillet, skinned
50ml./2 fl.oz. white wine
225ml./8 fl.oz. water
150g./5oz. large prawns
2 hard-boiled eggs, quartered
4 scallops, optional
275ml./^{1}/$_2$pt. (approx.) of milk
75g./3oz. butter
2 tablespoons of cream
50g./2oz. flour
Chopped dill or tarragon
Juice of ^{1}/$_2$ lemon, optional
900 g./2lbs. potatoes, peeled and cut into chunks
25g./1oz. of finely grated Cheddar cheese (optional)

Serves 4

1. Pre-heat oven to 200°C, Gas Mark 5. Shelf above centre.
2. Cut the fish fillets into large chunks and arrange in a baking dish with the white wine and water. Cover the dish with foil and place in the oven for about 15 minutes until the fish is only just cooked. Drain off and save the cooking liquor.
3. Arrange the cooked fish in a 1^1/$_2$ litre/2^1/$_2$ pint baking dish. Top with the prawns, hard boiled eggs, and scallops, if using.
4. Measure the reserved cooking liquor and make it up to 600ml./1 pint with milk. Pour this into a heavy saucepan, add 50g./2oz. of the butter and flour then, using a balloon whisk, stir the sauce continuously over a medium heat until it has come to the boil and is thick, smooth and creamy. Stir in the herbs, lemon juice and cream and, if using them, the salt and pepper. Pour this sauce over the fish and leave aside to cool.

6. Cook the potatoes until soft, then drain well and mash them with the remaining butter and sufficient milk to make them soft and creamy. Season well. Spread the mash over the fish, fork attractively, scatter with the cheese and bake the pie in the hot oven for 30-40 minutes.

This dish is good with French beans, frozen peas or a salad.

Cook's comment: Finely chopped capers and/or chopped anchovy fillets are a good addition to the sauce. Instead of milk and butter the mash is good made with olive oil, crushed garlic and a little milk to bring it to the right consistency. To make life easier, the pie can be made into a one-dish meal if 700g./1$^{1}/_{2}$ lb. of spinach is cooked, well-drained and arranged in the bottom of the buttered baking dish before the fish is added.

SMOKED HADDOCK AND PRAWN FLAN

375g./14oz. packet of frozen short crust pastry
1 medium onion, finely chopped
275 fl.oz./$^1/_2$ pt. milk
50g./2oz. flour
200g./7oz. shelled prawns
350g./12oz. smoked haddock fillets
Salt and pepper
2 heaped teaspoons of crème fraiche
25g./1oz. butter

Serves 4

1. Pre-heat the oven to 200°C, Gas Mark 5 – centre shelf
2. Roll out the defrosted pastry and put into a greased flan tin. Prick it and cover with foil and cook it for 20 minutes.
3. Fry the onion and keep.
4. Make a thick white sauce, by putting the milk, butter and flour into a heavy saucepan and, stirring the sauce continuously, whisking it with a balloon whisk. Season well, but without too much salt because of the salty fish to be added.
5. Poach the haddock in some water until cooked, drain, and then skin them and make certain there are no bones. Then flake into fairly small pieces.
6. Add onion, haddock, and prawns to the white sauce; then add crème fraiche and turn into the cooked pastry case.
7. Turn the oven down to 150°C, Gas Mark 2 and put the flan at the bottom of the oven.

Cook's comment: This is a very delicious, but rich lunch dish. It would be nice served with a green salad or frozen peas. If you are having to wait for a long time before you eat, turn the oven down to really low.

MEAT

Pasticcio

110g./4oz. onion, chopped
3 tablespoons of cooking oil
110g./4oz. minced pork
225g./8oz. minced beef, or all beef (12ozs)
225g./8oz. tinned tomatoes
$^1/_2$ level teaspoon dried oregano
1 clove of garlic, crushed (optional)
salt and pepper
225g./8oz. macaroni
40g./1$^1/_2$oz. butter
425ml./$^3/_4$pt. milk
40g./1$^1/_2$oz. flour
Grated nutmeg
110g./4oz. English Cheddar cheese, grated
Sprig of watercress to garnish
1 egg
5 fl.oz./$^1/_4$pt. single cream (or the equivalent in plain yoghourt)

Serves 4, but there may well be enough for second helpings!

1. Fry the chopped onion gently in the oil until soft then add
   the minced meat and stir over a high heat until starting to
   brown.
2. Remove pan from heat and stir in the tinned tomatoes
   with their juice, oregano and garlic. Cook for about 40
   minutes then season well to taste with salt and pepper.
3. Bring a large pan of salted water to the boil, add the
   macaroni and cook for about 10 minutes until just tender.
   Drain well.
4. Preheat a moderately hot oven 190°C, Gas Mark 5 – centre
   shelf.
5. Combine the remaining butter in a saucepan with the milk
   and the flour. Stir, vigorously, over a medium heat with a
   wire whisk or wooden spoon until the sauce is thick.

6. Remove the pan from the heat and season to taste with salt, pepper and nutmeg.
7. Stir 2 tablespoons of the sauce into the meat mixture.
8. Arrange half the macaroni in a layer in the bottom of a baking dish and sprinkle with 25g./1oz. of the grated cheese.
9. Spoon the meat over the macaroni then top with the remaining macaroni.
10. Beat the egg, stir in the cream or yoghourt, then stir this mixture into the sauce. Adjust seasoning to taste and pour over the macaroni. Top with the remaining cheese.
11. Bake the dish for about 35 minutes until golden brown and bubbling. Good served with a salad.

Cook's comment: This is an economical and adaptable dish. Traditionally made with macaroni; however, for a change, make it with spaghetti and layer in (with the meat) plenty of fried mushrooms or blanched and chopped courgettes or marrow. You can, of course, use left over roast meat instead of mince.

IDA'S FRIKADELLERS
(DANISH MEAT BALLS)

500g. minced meat, either fresh lamb or, half pork/
half lean beef
1 grated red onion
1-2 cloves crushed garlic
2-3 tablespoons herbs (for lamb, thyme and mint; for
pork/beef, oregano, parsley or basil)
Salt and pepper
1 egg
5 tablespoons flour
$2^1/_2$ litre/$1^1/_2$pts. milk
Oil and butter for frying

Serves 4, but there may be second helpings!

1. Mix all ingredients well together and leave in the fridge for
   at least 2 hours.
2. Stir well before frying – if a little heavy, add some water.
3. Use a tablespoon to form the meat balls.
4. Fry in oil and butter, 4 minutes each side.

Cook's comment: These Frikadeller are now very popular in
England, but my Danish friend who gave me this recipe
assures me that this is her very own adaptation!

Lasagne

125g./4oz. onion chopped finely
125g./4oz. streaky bacon cut up into small pieces
1$\frac{1}{2}$ tablespoons of cooking oil
1 clove of garlic crushed
225g./8oz. minced beef or packet minced Quorn
Salt and pepper
75g./3oz. butter
570ml./1 pint milk
50g./2oz. flour
225g./8oz. Cheddar cheese grated
225g./8oz. tinned tomatoes
Good tablespoon tomato purée
$\frac{1}{2}$ level teaspoon dried mixed herbs
1 pkt lasagne sheets, no pre-cooking required

Serves 4-6, depending on everyone's appetite!

1. Fry the onion and garlic gently in the oil until soft, preferably using a large frying pan or a casserole that can be used on top of the oven as well as inside, and then add the chopped bacon until starting to brown.
2. Add the minced beef to this until it, too, browns (if using the Quorn it can be added after the tomatoes).
3. Combine the butter in a heavy saucepan with the milk and the flour. Over a medium heat stir it vigorously with a balloon whisk until it is thick. Put half of the grated cheese into the sauce, reserving the remainder of the cheese.
4. To the bacon and onion and mince mixture add the tomatoes (and the Quorn if using). Stir in the tomato purée, the salt and pepper and the herbs, and continue to cook, stirring occasionally to make certain that it doesn't stick, for about 30 minutes.
5. Pre-heat a moderately hot oven 190ºC, Gas Mark 5. Centre shelf.
6. Place as many sheets of the lasagne as will fit comfortably into a square or oblong greased oven-proof dish and then

add about one half of the meat mixture. Then pour on one third of the cheese sauce. Put down another layer of the lasagne, then the rest of the meat mixture and cover it with the final layer of lasagne and then the rest of the cheese sauce. Finally top the prepared lasagne with the remainder of the grated cheese.

7. Put into the oven for 30 minutes or until the cheese is bubbling and brown. If your guests are delayed, you can leave the lasagne in a cooler oven.

Cook's comment: I have found that you can change this lasagne completely. Instead of the meat mixture you could make a melange of chopped ham, fried leeks and courgettes. Or flaked smoked haddock and a less cheesy sauce is very good. Experiments are the spice of life, and also of bridge lunches!

CHICKEN CHORIZO AND LENTIL ONE-POT CASSEROLE

175g./6oz. Chorizo sausage, cut into large cubes
6-8 boned chicken thighs
Oil
175g./6oz. onion, chopped
10g./^{1}/$_2$oz. flour
400g. tin of chopped tomatoes (and their juice)
2 tablespoons of tomato puree
275ml./^{1}/$_2$pint of chicken stock
3 sprigs of thyme and 1 bay leaf
Salt and pepper
225g/8oz. baby potatoes cut in half
125gm/4oz. Puy lentils (rinsed in cold water)
200g./7oz. fresh baby spinach leaves

Serves 4

1. Pre-heat the oven to 150°C, Gas Mark 2. Centre shelf.
2. Place the Chorizo sausage in a large heavy frying pan and fry it gently for about five minutes, without added fat, to draw out the oil, then lift it out into an ovenproof casserole.
3. Add the chicken to the frying pan and slowly brown it all over in the oil from the chorizo sausage adding a little more oil if necessary, then remove it into the casserole.
4. Now cook the onion gently in the pan until it is soft then blend in the flour, canned tomatoes, tomato puree, stock, thyme and bay leaf. Bring to the boil, stirring, then season well with salt and pepper and tip the pan contents into the casserole also adding the potatoes and lentils.
5. Cover the casserole and cook for about 40 minutes until the chicken is almost cooked. Add the spinach and cook for a further 5 minutes or so, when the chicken should be completely cooked through and the spinach barely soft. Ladle into large soup plates to serve.

Cook's comment: The casserole cooks slowly, so it won't matter if it's left in the oven for quite a bit longer; just whizz into the kitchen and stir in the spinach so it has time to cook while your future Bridge players get settled at the table. Instead of the potatoes, or in addition, try adding a 400g./14oz. can of drained chick peas.

If you own a slow cooker, cook for 3 hours on high.

MOUSSAKA

350g./12oz. aubergines
350g./12oz. potatoes
3 tablespoons of cooking oil
100g./4oz. butter
1 large onion, finely sliced
2 cloves garlic, finely chopped (optional)
450g./1lb. cooked lamb, minced or processed
2 x 225g./2 x 8oz. tin tomatoes
25 g./1oz. flour
275ml./$^{1}/_{2}$ pint milk
50g./2oz. cheddar cheese, grated
Salt and pepper
250g./9oz. Greek yoghourt
1 egg beaten
25g./1oz. Parmesan cheese, grated

Serves 4

1. Pre-heat the oven to 180ºC, Gas Mark 4. Centre shelf.
2. Slice the unpeeled aubergine and peel and slice the potatoes. Fry until soft in the oil and 50g./2oz. of the butter. Remove from the pan.
3. Melt 25g./1oz. butter in the pan and fry the sliced onion. When soft add the finely chopped garlic, minced meat and the tinned tomatoes and their juice. Mix together and season well with salt and pepper.
4. Line a buttered shallow pie dish (or medium sized roasting pan) with the sliced aubergine and potatoes. Spread with the meat mixture.
5. Combine the remaining 25g./1oz. butter in a heavy saucepan with the flour and milk. Using a balloon whisk, beat over a medium heat until the sauce is smooth and thick. Remove from the heat, stir in the cheddar cheese, cool, then mix in the yoghourt and beaten egg.
Season well for taste with salt and pepper.

6. Spread the sauce over the top of the meat mixture and sprinkle evenly with the Parmesan cheese.
7. Bake the Moussaka in the centre of the pre-heated oven for about 1 hour.

Cook's comment: Good with a green salad tossed with black olive dressing (chopped, de-stoned olives added to a vinaigrette).

700g./1¹/₂lbs. of aubergines, instead of potatoes, can be used. A good dish in which to use cold roast lamb.

QUICK CASSOULET

2 duck leg joints
225g./8oz. garlic sausage, cut into chunky dice or 4 meaty pork sausages
2 tablespoons goose fat or oil
125g./4 oz. streaky bacon, shredded
125g./4 oz. onion, chopped
3 cloves of garlic, crushed
1 level tablespoon flour
400g./12oz. can chopped tomatoes
2 or 3 x 450g./1lb. cans cannellini beans
Few sprigs of thyme
350ml./12fl.oz. stock
50ml./2 fl.oz. white wine
Salt, pepper

Serves 4

1. Pre-heat oven 180°C, Gas mark 4. Centre shelf.
2. Cut each duck leg in two to make 4 joints in total. Place the duck joints and sausage in a heavy frying pan, with the goose fat or oil, and fry for about 5 minutes until brown on all sides. Then place the joints and sausages in a large oven-proof casserole.

3. Add the prepared bacon, onion and garlic to the frying pan. Cook until the onion is soft and lightly browned, then blend in the flour, canned tomatoes (including the juice), thyme, wine and stock. Bring this mixture to the boil, stirring, then season well with salt and pepper.
4. Drain the cans of cannellini beans into a sieve, rinse in cold water, then stir into the contents of the frying pan. Bring to the boil and check the seasoning again before tipping the whole lot into the casserole, with the duck and sausages. Cover the casserole and place in the oven for about 50 minutes.

Cook's comment: Serve the cassoulet in large soup plates with a well-dressed salad on the side. Cassoulet is a very amenable dish as, if you lower the temperature, it will happily wait until you are ready for it. A little more stock may be added if necessary, or remove the lid and increase the oven temperature if the liquid needs reducing. Chicken legs and other types of beans can be used as alternatives. Cassoulet needs a lot of seasoning, so always check for this before serving.

Chicken Myers

200ml./7fl.oz. half fat crème fraiche
4-6 boned chicken thighs cut into chunks
225g./8oz. packet of frozen broccoli, thawed
280g./10^1/$_2$fl.oz. can condensed cream of chicken soup
4 rounded tablespoons mayonnaise
^{1}/$_2$ level teaspoon curry powder
50g./2oz. Cheddar cheese, grated

Serves 4

1. Preheat a moderately hot over 190ºC, Gas Mark 5. Centre shelf.
2. Arrange the chicken and broccoli in a shallow baking dish.
3. Combine the undiluted chicken soup with the mayonnaise, cream and curry powder. Spoon this over the chicken and broccoli then sprinkle with the grated cheese.
4. Bake in the preheated oven for about 30 minutes until the chicken is cooked through and the cheese is turning golden brown.

Cook's comment: Prepared in minutes – but you would never think so. When you try the subtle flavour of this dish you would think it had taken time to achieve it.
Serve with potatoes or boiled rice.

TARRAGON LAMB

680g./1¹/2lbs. lamb neck fillets
1 tablespoonful olive oil
1 large onion or 6 shallots
2 cloves garlic
170g./6oz. chestnut mushrooms
150ml/^{1}/4pt. light stock
1 teaspoon soy sauce
110g./4 oz. crème fraiche
Salt and black pepper to season
1 teaspoon dried tarragon

Serves 4

1. Preheat the oven to 180°C, Gas Mark 4.
2. Peel and finely chop the onion or shallots and garlic.
3. Trim any fat off the meat and cut into slices about 2cm./^{3}/4in.thick.
4. Wash, dry, and quarter the mushrooms.
5. Heat the olive oil in an ovenproof casserole.
6. Gently sauté the onion and garlic until soft.
7. Add the tarragon and mushrooms. Return to the heat for 1-2 minutes then add soy sauce and stock.
8. Place in the oven for 1 hour.
9. Adjust seasoning to taste.
10. Stir in the crème fraiche just before serving.

Cook's comments: Serve with long grain rice and seasonal vegetables or salad.

VENISON CASSEROLE

1kg./approx. 2¹/₂lbs. venison cut into small chunks
(discarding sinew etc.)
Oil (olive or sunflower)
175g./6oz. lean, streaky bacon (shredded)
225g./8oz. mushrooms cut into quarters
450g./1lb. onions, chopped
50g./2oz. flour
10fl.oz./¹/₂pt. red wine
12 stoned prunes, chopped
850fl.oz./1¹/₂pts. stock (or 2 stock cubes made up with
equivalent water)

Serves 8 (for 4 people, halve the ingredients).

1. Heat the oven to 150°C, Gas Mark 2.
2. In a large oven-proof casserole, fry the onion until soft in a
    little of the oil, then continue to fry adding the bacon and
    then the mushrooms. Take all of them out and put on a plate.
3. In the same casserole, batch fry the diced venison, adding
    the oil as necessary, until it is all browned.
4. Return the onions, bacon and mushrooms to the casserole
    and blend in the flour and then the wine and stock. Season
    well and add the prunes.
5. Cover the casserole and put in the oven on the lowest shelf
    for 2 hours.

Cook's comment: This can be pre-cooked and when it is
required reheat at 170°C, Gas Mark 3, adding, if you would
like, cooked potatoes for the last ¹/₂ hour. Check the seasoning
before serving and garnish with chopped parsley.

I would suggest that, if you have not used frozen venison, you
could freeze half of this casserole and use again within the
month.

Casseroles, in the winter, are a great stand-by. They can be cooked in a slow cooker very successfully, or in a low to medium oven and they don't seem to mind being left in until you and your guests are quite ready to eat.

Other variations which you could try might be:

Pork with apricots and a little cinnamon;
Lamb with sliced apples or olives; Chicken with orange.
Adding some crème fraiche at the end gives casseroles an extra something.

PUDDINGS OR DESSERTS

We have come to the conclusion that puddings are generally superfluous – taking up too much valuable time before we can settle down to tackle those cards. Cheese and biscuits or fruit are generally quite enough before you offer the coffee and those all-important chocolates or mints!

However, there are times, particularly if it is an evening event, when a two, or even three-course meal would be appropriate.

LEMON ICICLE

2 medium eggs, separated
50g./2oz. caster sugar
150ml./¹/₄pt. fresh double cream
Finely grated rind and juice of 1 lemon

Serves 4

1. Whisk the egg whites until they are very stiff, then gradually add the sugar, whisking well after each addition until the mixture is very thick.
2. Whip the cream until softly thick, stir in the egg yolks, then fold the mixture evenly into the whisked whites, along with the lemon rind and juice.
3. Pour the mixture into a lined small loaf tin 750ml.1¹/₂pt. capacity and freeze until firm.
4. Turn the lemon cream out of the loaf tin, wrap and re-freeze until ready to serve.

Cook's comment: The Lemon Icicle may be frozen for 2-3 months. Remove it from the freezer for at least 10 minutes before serving for the flavour to develop and to allow it to soften slightly for slicing.

RAW APPLE DESSERT

100g./4oz.apples, preferably Coxes
200g.7oz. meringues (either bought or home-made), crushed
150ml./^{1}/4pt. whipping cream
125g./4^1/2ozs. dark chocolate, broken into small pieces and
roughly grated

Serves 4

1. Grate the apples roughly and place in a deep dish in layers
   with the meringues, starting with apples and finishing with
   the meringues. Make at least two layers.
2. Decorate with whipped cream on top and roughly cover
   with bits of chocolate.

Cook's comment: As the meringues have to be crushed it
doesn't really matter whether they are bought ones. It is
important to completely cover the apples with the meringues
and then the cream, or they will go brown.

SURPRISE APPLE SNOW

3 or 4 bought individual sponge cakes
2 large eggs
250 ml./^{1}/$_2$ pint milk
25g./1oz. granulated sugar
4 large cooking or eating apples
Vanilla pod
110g./4oz. raspberries
2 tablespoons honey
110g/4oz. caster sugar
2 tablespoons calvados
Juice of a lemon

Serves 4

1. Peel, core and slice the apples into a flameproof bowl with the juice of half a lemon.
2. Cover the bowl and microwave for 3 minutes or until apples are soft and can be mashed easily (cooking time depends on variety of apple so it is better to cook for a minute at a time until apples are really soft).
3. Set apples to cool.
4. Mix the honey and raspberries (reserve a few of the raspberries for decoration) in a flameproof basin and microwave for 1-2 minutes until the raspberries are soft.
5. Place the sponge cakes in the bottom of the serving bowl (or one in each of 4 individual dishes if preferred).
6. Spoon the raspberry mixture over the sponge cakes and leave to cool.
7. Heat the milk, granulated sugar and vanilla pod very gently, separate the eggs and add the yolks to the warm milk stirring all the time.
8. Stir until thickened but do not allow to boil, remove from the heat and take out the vanilla pod.
9. Spoon the custard carefully over the raspberry mixture and leave to cool.

10. Put the cooked and cooled apples into a blender with the caster sugar and the rest of the lemon juice and blend into a smooth puree.
11. Beat the egg whites until really stiff, then slowly fold in the apple puree and calvados. Mix carefully and spoon on top of the custard/raspberries.
12. Chill for several hours and serve decorated with a few uncooked raspberries.

Cook's comment: This will take a bit more time than most of the recipes in this book, but it is certainly worth it!

If you don't have a microwave, cook the apples and then the honey and raspberries in saucepans on the stove.

RAISIN, RUM AND NUT PIE

225g./8oz. seeded raisins
175ml./6fl.oz. boiling water
75g./3oz. caster sugar
1^1/$_2$ level tablespoons of cornflour
^{1}/$_4$ level teaspoon of salt
Rind and juice of ^{1}/$_2$ lemon
Rind and juice of ^{1}/$_2$ orange
50g./2oz. chopped walnuts
50g./2oz. green grapes, halved and pips removed
75g./3oz. butter
175g./6oz. digestive biscuit crumbs
1 tablespoon of rum (or rum essence to taste)
1 teaspoon of Demerara sugar

Serves 4-6 generously

1. Place the raisins in a saucepan and cover with the boiling water. Simmer gently for about 5 minutes.
2. Mix the sugar with the cornflour and salt; stir this into the raisin mixture. Bring to the boil then add fruit juice and continue to cook until thick, stirring.
3. Remove the pan from the heat and add the orange and lemon rind and juice, then leave aside to cool before stirring in the chopped walnuts and grapes.
4. Melt the butter, stir in the digestive biscuit crumbs until they are well coated in butter. Pat the biscuit crumbs into the base and sides of an oval flan dish.
5. Spread the raisin mixture over the crumb crust.
6. Whip the cream with rum until thick then spread over the top of the raisin mixture and scatter with the Demerara sugar.

Cook's comment: This is very delicious, but very rich. If you have any guests who are anti-alcohol, just omit the rum.

HAMPTON COURT TART

150ml./¼pt. fresh single cream
200g./7oz. packet puff pastry
50g./2oz. butter
225g./8oz. cottage cheese
50g./2oz. ground rice
125g./4oz. caster sugar
50g./2oz. sultanas
Grated rind and juice of a large lemon
2 medium eggs, separated

Serves 4, with some left over.

1. Preheat a moderately hot oven, 190°C, Gas Mark 5. Shelf above centre.
2. Roll out the puff pastry and use it to line a 20-23 cm./8-9in. flan tin. Prick the base.
3. Melt the butter in a fairly large saucepan. Remove from the heat and cool a little before adding the cottage cheese, ground rice, sugar, sultanas, lemon rind and juice, cream and egg yolks. Stir together.
4. Whisk the egg whites stiffly and gently fold them evenly into the mixture in the pan.
5. Turn the mixture into the pastry case, lightly spread it level, then bake the tart in the preheated oven for about 40 minutes until the top is golden brown and the pastry is cooked.

Cook's comment: This can be served hot or cold. If your guests haven't been too greedy, and you have had it as a hot pudding, it can be served as a delicious cake on another occasion, although obviously within a day or two because of the cream.

FRUIT IN A CLOUD

450g./1lb. soft fruit, chopped
125g./4oz. Greek Yoghourt
125g./4oz. fromage frais
50g./2oz. Muscovy brown sugar

Serves 4

1. Put the yoghourt and the fromage frais into a bowl and mix them well.
2. Add the fruit to the bowl, and mix together.
3. Spoon the mélange into 4 glasses and just before serving scatter with a good layer of the sugar.

Cook's comment: This is so easy that I hesitate to put it into the book. It is, however, extremely useful if you are at a loss for a pudding. Any soft fruit could be used: strawberries, raspberries, blueberries, nectarines, cooked dried apricots – the list is endless – experiment!

Of course, you could simply omit everything but the fruit and change your pudding into a delicious fruit salad, which is always greatly enjoyed by practically everybody.

TEAS

Things to buy: It's not cheating, just being sensible, and these are all delicious! Crumpets, a malt loaf, Danish pastries, toasted tea-cakes.

On the other hand, sandwiches are always popular:

Sardine and cream cheese
cream cheese and stem ginger
herbs and cheese and chutney
ham minced up with chutney
smoked salmon and crème fraich
chopped chicken with mayonnaise, walnuts and lemon juice
cream cheese and chopped watercress or rocket
chopped dessert apple, mayonnaise and chopped walnuts
and that perennial favourite, cucumber

and any other filling that you think would please your guests. Remember that the bread for these sandwiches is important; I would suggest that sometimes you try granary brown sliced very thinly, or a very fresh bap cut in half.

Scones

1 egg
275g./10oz. self raising flour
75ml./3fl.oz. single cream
100ml./4fl.oz. milk
Sultanas (optional)

1. Pre-heat oven to 200ºC, Gas Mark 6.
2. Put the flour into a bowl and break in the egg. Pour in the cream and milk and mix together lightly to form a smooth dough.
3. If a little soggy, add more flour and if too dry, add a little more milk.
4. Add sultanas, if desired.
5. Pat the dough out to about 1.5cm./1/2inch thick. Cut into rounds or squares.
6. Place scones on a lightly greased baking sheet. Brush the tops with milk and bake in the centre shelf of a pre-heated oven for 10-12 minutes. Cool on a wire rack.

Cook's comment: These are, I am assured, infallible and quite delicious. They can, of course, be served with cream and jam, in which case, you probably would not need anything else for your guests' tea.

MOTHER'S GINGER CAKE

225g./8oz. self raising flour
225g./8oz. butter
225g./8oz. caster sugar
3 eggs
110g./4oz. ground almonds
2 tablespoons milk
Chopped preserved ginger and juice (as much or as little as you think)
Few cubes of crystallised ginger, chopped finely

1. Pre-heat the oven to 150ºC, Gas Mark 2.
2. Mix the sugar, butter, flour and eggs; then fold in the ground almonds and the 2 tablespoons of milk and add all the ginger.
3. Put in a greased loaf tin and bake in the middle of the oven for 1 hour and 15 minutes.

Cook's comment: This keeps extremely well and is delicious either served on its own or sliced thinly and spread with butter.
It can be frozen.

EASY DATE LOAF

225g./8oz. stoned dates, chopped
225ml./8fl.oz. boiling water
125g./4oz. caster sugar
1 egg, beaten
250g./9oz. self-raising flour
1 level teaspoon of baking powder

Serves 4, and then again!

1. Pre-heat the oven to 180ºC, Gas Mark 4. Centre shelf.
2. Soak the chopped dates in the boiling water for 10 minutes.
3. Add all the remaining ingredients and mix well.
4. Spoon into a lined loaf tin.
5. Put into the pre-heated oven and bake for 45 minutes. Allow to cool, then turn out.

Cook's comment: As you can see, this is a really easy cake and very moist and delicious. It keeps well in a tin with a well-fitting lid, or could even be frozen and defrosted when it was needed.

GOOEY CHOCOLATE CAKE

125g./4oz. plain dessert chocolate, broken into pieces
125g./4oz. butter at room temperature
125g./4oz. caster sugar
3 eggs separated
50g./2oz. ground almonds
$1/4$ teaspoon of almond essence
50g./2oz. plain flour
Sifted icing sugar
225-275ml./8-10fl.oz. fresh double cream
350-450g./12oz.-1lb. of strawberries

Serves 8. To make it suitable for your Bridge foursome, simply halve the ingredients.

1. Pre-heat the oven to 180°, Gas Mark 4, centre shelf. Grease a 20cm./8in. cake tin and dust with caster sugar.
2. Place 2 tablespoons of water and the chocolate into a basin, resting over a pan of hot water. Heat very gently until the chocolate has melted. Cool.
3. Meanwhile cream the butter with the sugar until it is very soft, fluffy and paler in colour. Beat in the egg yolks, one at a time beating well after each yolk is added.
4. Whisk the egg whites until very stiff.
5. Fold the melted chocolate into the creamed mixture, then the ground almonds and almond essence.
6. Fold in a rounded tablespoon of the whisked egg whites, then mix in the flour and, finally, fold in the remaining whisked whites until all are evenly blended. Spread the mixture lightly and smoothly into the prepared tin.
7. Bake the cake for about 35 minutes or until the outer edge is firm and springy, but the very centre of the cake remains slightly soft.
8. Cool the cake slightly in the tin, then turn it out onto a wire rack and leave until cold before dusting with icing sugar.
9. Either serve the cake just dusted with icing sugar and with a bowl of the whipped cream and the strawberries to

dollop on each portion; or cut the cake carefully into 3 layers and then sandwich them together again with sliced, sugared strawberries and whipped cream, reserving the best 5-6 strawberries and some cream to decorate the top.

Cook's comment: The secret of this delicious gooey cake simply lies in taking great care not to cook it too much. It makes a good pudding too, particularly when served with strawberries and a bowl of Greek yoghourt or whipped cream.

Appendix 1
Bidding Aid

Points	Opening Bid	Partner's 1st Response	Opener's 2nd Bid
12–14 pts. Balanced hand. No 5 card major	1 No Trump	0–10 points, bid 2 of 5 card suit	No bid
12–14 points. Balanced hand. No 5 card major	1 No Trump	11+ pt bid 3 of 5 card suit 0–9 pts, balanced, No Bid 10/12 pts, balanced, 2 NT. 13–18 pts, balanced, 3 NT. 19+ pts, balanced, 4 NT.	Appropriate to Response and dependent on whether 1 No Trump was 12 or 14 points.
15–19 pts. Balanced hand. No 5 card major	Call lower 4 card suit*	Reply with 6+ pts.	15/16 pts. 1 NT 17/18 pts. 2 NT 19 pts. 3 NT
20–22pts, and balanced hand	2 No Trumps	With 4+pts balanced, 3 NT With 5 card suit, bid the suit.	Dependent on response
12–18 pts. & 4 or 5 card suit, & 7 or less Losing Tricks	1 of at least a 4 card suit.	6–15pts, bid new suit at same level, (i.e. 1H/1S) 9–15pts, bid new suit at next level. (i.e. 1H to 2D) 6–9pts, balanced hand 1NT, 10/12pts, bid 2NT. 13–18pts, bid 3NT. 6/9pts & 4 of opener's suit 2 of same suit, 10+pts & 4 of opener's suit, bid 3 of same suit. 16+pts, jump shift into new suit. Any change of suit is forcing.	12–15pts bid 2 of opening suit if you hold 5 of them, or 15–19pts bid 1NT, or agree partner's suit, or Jump in own original suit, if particularly good or long, or 4NT, if a Slam is possible, and agreeing last bid suit.
19–22 pts with at least 4 of a suit, and 4 or less Losing Tricks.	Bid 2 of a suit	Must reply. 2NT with under 4pts, otherwise, support opener's suit, or bid own best suit.	With 5 of the bid suit, repeat it, or support partner's suit, or offer another suit or No Trump

Points	Opening Bid	Partner's 1st Response	Opener's 2nd Bid
23+ pts, and 4 or less Losers	2 Clubs	Must reply, and be kept open for at least 2 rounds, preferably to game. Bid 2 of best suit, or 2 NT. With under 3 pts, bid negative 2D.	Support partner's suit, or bid your own, or NT. After 2 D response, with a balanced hand and 23/24 pts bid 2 NT; with 25+ pts and balanced hand, bid 3 NT. Otherwise, bid your own suit, jumping if necessary **Partner's 2nd Response** Continue bidding, unless you have absolute minimum points and opener has rebid 2 NT, in which case you could say No bid.
Pre-empt with 6–10pts and 7 of one suit	Open 3 of the long suit	Put up in the long suit with at least 10 points and 2 of opener's long suit. Change to a new suit with 16+pts (Opponents must have good opening hand and 5 or 6 card suit to enter the bidding)	Appropriate to response
Pre-empt with 11+pts and 7 of one a suit	1 of the long suit	According to hand	Jump in long suit
	Blackwood Having decided on the suit in which one wishes to try for a Slam, ask for Aces by bidding 4 No Trumps.	5 Clubs = 0 or 4 Aces 5 Diamonds = 1 Ace 5 Hearts = 2 Aces 5 Spades = 3 Aces	Either return to desired suit, bidding 5 of it if possible. Or, continue by asking for Kings bidding 5 No Trumps **Partner's 2nd Response** 6 Clubs = 0 or 4 Kings 6 Diamonds = 1 King 6 Hearts = 2 Kings 6 Spades = 3 Kings **Opener's 3rd Bid** Return to the suit in which you wish to play, bidding a Small or Grand Slam.

DOUBLING			
Opponent's	Your Bid	Intervening Opponent Bid	Your Partner's Bid
1 No Trump	With 16+ points, say, 'Double.' This is a 'Penalty Double.'	1) No Bid .... 2) If bid made	1) Only reply if you hold a very poor hand, under 6 points and long suit. 2) If bid made by opponent, bid normally.
a) 1 Club, or 1 Diamond, or 1 Heart, or 1 Spade, b) opening with a pre-emptive 3 of a suit.	a) With 12 + points, and good cards in 3 suits, but not that bid by Opener, say 'Double.' This is a 'Take-Out Double,' asking for partner's best suit. b) with 16+ points do a Take-Out Double		Bid best suit. With 0–8 points, bid at normal level. With 9–12 points, jump bid. With 13+ points go to game level.
Has reached a Game call	Double for penalties, meaning you don't think your opponents can make their contract.	Could change the suit, or redouble	Probably No Bid, but may also Double if suit has been changed.

Key Counts		But:	
Game in 3 NT	needs 25/26pts	Losing Tricks are all important. You need 7 or less Losers to open, and 9 or less to reply at basic level. Always take away combined Losing Tricks from 18, which will give the potential number of tricks to be made.	**N.B.** Losing Trick Count does not work if the contract is in No Trumps.
Game in 4H/4S	needs 25/26pts		
Game in 5C/5D	needs 29pts		
Small Slam	needs 32–34pts		
Grand Slam	needs 37+pts		

The forerunner of this chart was designed by the late James Wilcox, an enthusiastic and dedicated player, and a very nice man.

* In strict Acol Bridge the higher of both 4 and 5 card suits is bid.

Appendix 2

Answers

Chapter 2

a) 1 No Trump (and then for your 2nd bid a Diamond)
b) 1 No Trump

QUIZ
  1. Player drawing highest card.
  2. 7 No Trumps.
  3. 4 Clubs.
  4. 1 Club.
  5. (a) 15 points;   (b) Yes, you can open.
  6. 9 tricks.
  7. 5 points.
  8. (a) Shuffling, or making   (b) Second pack is placed on your right.
  9. No.
  10. No.

Chapter 4
QUIZ
  1. Diamonds & Clubs.
  2. No, you could throw away a card you don't think will be useful.
  3. Clubs.
  4. They are the same, both scoring 30 points per trick.
  5. Less than 100 points. Yes, provided the opposition has not made a game in between.
  6. Overtricks, or points for opponents not making their contract; or bonus points.
  7. You will have scored 120 points below the line, therefore a game, but can carry nothing forward.
  8. 60 below, 20 above.

9. No.

10. 27 – own hand, dummy's hand, plus opening lead.

Scoring Quiz Answers

1. N/S have bid 11 tricks, but they only made 8. E/W score 50 x 3 = 150 above the line.

2. E/W bid 3 NT and made 10 tricks. They score 40 + 30 + 30 = 100 (a game) below the line which makes them vulnerable. They also score 1 x 30 = 30 above the line for the extra trick.

3. N/S bid 10 tricks and only made 9. E/W score 1 x 50 = 50 points above the line, as N/S are still non-vulnerable.

4. N/S bid 11 tricks and only made 7. E/W score 4 x 50 = 200 points above the line.

5. E/W bid 10 tricks and only made 8. N/S score 2 x 100 = 200 points above the line (because E/W are vulnerable).

6. N/S bid 10 tricks and made 12. They score 4 x 30 = 120 below the line; this is a game, so they are now also vulnerable. They also score 2 x 30 = 60 above the line.

7. N/S bid 8 tricks and made 9. They score 2 x 30 = 60 below the line and 1 x 30 = 30 above the line.

8. E/W bid 10 tricks and only made 6. As they are vulnerable, N/S score 4 x 100 = 400 above the line.

9. E/W bid 7 tricks and only made 5. N/S score 2 x 100 = 200 above the line.

10. N/S bid 11 tricks and made 12. They score 5 x 20 = 100 below the line, which is added to the 60 they already have; and 1 x 20 above the line. They have now won two games out of the three, so score an additional 500 points above the line. N/S scored 1690 points and E/W 630 points, therefore N/S has 1,030 points, which count as + 10 to N/S, because 950-1040 = 10 points; 1050-1140 = 11 points, etc.

Chapter 5
QUIZ

1. (a) She has 12+ points, but not much more, as she has merely responded 2 Hearts; you know that your partner has at least 5 Hearts.
2. Only 9 tricks are required.
3. Both partners being relatively poor in the same suit; and the opponents being able to get into that long suit.
4. 40 below; 30 above.
5. (a) Yes; (b) Hearts, because you only have two in that suit.
6. (a) 40 points; (b) No;   Yes;   Yes.
7. (a) 9 points; (b) these are honours, you score 100 points above the line.
8. (a) Opponents must have at least 12+6; therefore your partnership can only have 22 points at the most; (b) No.
9. 3 No Trumps – but of course, you should have bid your Diamonds on your second bid, before you repeated your Hearts.
10. 200.

Chapter 6
QUIZ

1. 2 Clubs.
2. No bid, because the most you could have between you is 14+8=22 points, not enough for a game.

Chapter 7
QUIZ

1. 2 Hearts.
2. She has 4 Hearts, and 6-9 points – 'One up, shut up'. You could have 14+9 points at the most; not enough for a game in Hearts.
3. 2 No Trumps.

4. 2 Hearts, or 2 Spades.
5. 700 points above your line.
6. No, unless partner has 22 points!
7. 2 Hearts. You only have 15+9 at the most, not enough for a game, although it is tempting.
8. 200 points above your line.

Chapter 8
Revision Quiz
1. 8.
2. 29.
3. 6-9.
4. (a) No bid;   (b) a Heart.
5. 2 Diamonds (the Weakness Take-Out).
6. (a) 1 Club, (b) 2 No Trumps.
7. 300 points to your opponents, above the line.
8. 1 Heart; 2 Hearts; No bid, just bidding one-up in your partner's suit.
9. (a) 1 Spade, (b) 2 No Trumps.
10. A Heart.

Chapter 9
1. 6 Losing Tricks.
2. 7 Losing Tricks.
3. 6 Losing Tricks.
4. 4 Losing Tricks.

CHAPTER 14
Be brave and support the Clubs; you have only 7 losing tricks and your partner only 5 – you might get a slam.

Chapter 15
QUIZ
1. 2 No Trumps.
2. 300 points.
3. 10 of Clubs.
4. 6-9 points with even distribution.
5. (a) Yes. 1 NT.
    (b) otherwise as an over-caller, say No Bid, unless your partner has also made a bid, in which case you could respond to her with 2 NT.
6. (a) 2 Clubs; (b) No.
7. 15/16 points.
8. (a) 2 Diamonds to show your lack of points,
    (b) Spades to show your best suit.
9. 3 Clubs.
10. 1 Club, then on your next bid jump in the Clubs, to show you really like them.

Chapter 16
QUIZ
1. The 10 must be either a singleton or doubleton. The only missing higher cards in that suit are the Ace and Jack. If South had the Ace, he would have had to lead it; and if he held the Jack, it would have been the higher of touching Honours, so he could not have led the 10. MUD is not applicable. If it were a doubleton, the lower card must be the 7, 6, or 4, and therefore no possible danger.   North must have the Ace, and if this is not played, you would take the trick with your King or Queen, and not return that suit.
2. All the Honours are visible and also the cards below the 5 that was led; therefore, it cannot be bottom to an Honour, nor a doubleton, nor MUD – that 5 is a singleton.   So take the trick and then change suit in case you are trumped later.

3. South must have the Queen or his King is a singleton. Win the trick with your Ace, and then lead another suit, because you are fated to lose at least one more trick in that suit.

Which card should you lead in a suit contract?

1. **6** 2.
2. **7** 3.
3. 8 **5** 2.
4. 9 **6** 5 4.
5. 8 **5** 4 3 2.
6. **10** 9 3 2.
7. 10 6 3 **2.**
8. **J** 10.
9. J 9 **8.**
10. **Q** J 7 2.
11. J 9 7 **6.**
12. Q 10 5 **4.**
13. Q **10** 9.
14. **K** Q J 5.
15. K **J** 10 6 4.
16. **A** J 6 5 4.

Chapter 17
QUIZ
1. a) 200 points, b) 400 points.
2. 17-18 points.
3. 4 Diamonds.
4. 3 No Trumps.
5. a) 2 No Trumps; (b) No Bid.
6. 11+ points, the Strong Weakness Take-out.
7. The Ace of Hearts.
8. a) 2 Hearts, a positive bid; (b) 4 No Trumps – 'I agree Hearts, let's try for a Slam'.

Chapter 18
Doubling Scoring Quiz

1. North has bid 2 Spades and been doubled. He only makes 7 tricks (not 8); as he is non-vulnerable E/W score 100 points above the line.

2. West is non-vulnerable, she bids 3 Hearts, is doubled, and makes 10 tricks. She scores $3 \times 30 \times 2 = 180$ below the line and 50 for the 'insult', plus 100 for the doubled overtrick above the line.

3. East bids 4 Spades and is doubled. She only makes 6 tricks (not 10). As she is now vulnerable, she has to give N/S points above the line: for the 1st – 200, 2nd – 300, 3rd – 300, 4th – 300 = 1100 points.

4. South bids 2 Clubs and is doubled and makes 11 tricks (not 8). He is still non-vulnerable. He gets $20 \times 2 \times 2 = 80$ below the line and $100 \times 3 = 300$ for the overtricks + 50 for the 'insult' above the line.

5. North bids 3 Hearts and is doubled and only makes 5 tricks (not 9). He is still non-vulnerable, so E/W gain points above the line: for the 1st – 100, 2nd – 200, 3rd – 200, 4th – 300 = 800 points.

6. West bids 6 Clubs and is doubled. She makes 13 tricks. She scores $6 \times 20 \times 2 = 240$ points below the line, and above the line 50 for the 'insult' + 200 for the overtrick vulnerable + 750 for the vulnerable Small Slam, which she had contracted to make. She has won 2 games and the Rubber, so gains an extra 700 for 2 clear games.

E/W score a total of 3170 points.
N/S scores a total of 1540 points.
Therefore, E/W has won the rubber by 1630 points = + 16.

Chapter 19
1. (a) No Bid; (b) double for penalties.
2. (a) Do a take-out double; (b) bid 4 Hearts, because you know she has 9 – 12 points, as she made a jump bid.
3. Yes, you should double, as you have a minimum of 20 points between you, and they can, therefore, only have 20 points at the most.
4. 500 points.
5. (a) She has an opening hand that is poor in Spades and good in the other 3 suits.
   (b) Bid 1 No Trump, you have 6/9 points and a stopper in Spades.
6. 120 below the line, and 50 above the line for the insult. They have doubled you into game.
7. No Bid. The final contract would be 1 No Trump doubled, poor opponents!

Chapter 21
QUIZ
1. 2 Diamonds.
2. No Bid.
3. 3 Clubs.
4. 1 No Trump to keep the bidding open and tell her your points count. You can't support her Hearts as you have only 3 of them. Wait to see what your partner will bid next.
5. 2 Clubs.
6. 2 Diamonds, which is a jump shift.
7. 3 No Trumps.
8. 1 No Trump.
9. 2 No Trumps.
10. No Bid.

INDEX